Contemporary Christian Social Concerns Series

General Editor: E. P. Smith

Volume One
Unemployment Under The Judgement of God
by Peter Mayhew

Volume Two
Rendering Unto Caesar
by
Antony Hurst

Volume Three
No Free Lunches
by John Brockett

RENDERING UNTO CAESAR

Towards a Framework for Integrating Paid Employment with Christian Belief

by
ANTONY HURST

CHURCHMAN PUBLISHING LIMITED
WORTHING : 1986

Rendering Unto Caesar
was first published by
Churchman Publishing Limited
117 Broomfield Avenue
Worthing
West Sussex BN14 7SF
in 1986

ISBN 1 85093 039 2

Distributed to the book trade by
Bailey Bros. & Swinfen Limited
Warner House
Folkestone
Kent CT19 6PH

Churchman's Agents in Canada
Jonathan Gould Books of Winnipeg

Typeset by CPJ Fotoset Limited of Worthing
and printed by Dorling Print Group of London

Contents

Preface

I am a civil servant in the Department of Health and Social Security and I am an ordained Priest of the Church of England. I enjoy my job even when the inevitable frustrations of working within a large institution are taken into account, and I feel right as a clergyman even though I suffer the inevitable doubts whether what I do is an adequate response to God's calling.

The origin of this book lies in two particular sets of experiences. The first set occurred when I found myself at the receiving end of the reactions of my civil service colleagues to the news that I had been accepted by ACCM and was about to embark upon ordination training. Most of them said first, "I suppose this means you will be leaving the Department and becoming a vicar"; I knew I didn't want to do this, but when I said so and made it clear that I intended exercising a ministry within the DHSS, they then asked, "What will you actually do?". I knew I would actually do something, but I found it impossible at that stage to articulate exactly what. This is a difficult position for anybody to be in, but it is a particularly difficult position for a civil servant for whom the articulation of policy is a stock in trade. What I did, therefore, was what all civil servants do when they are confused; I started putting something down on paper.

The second set of experiences happened simultaneously, though I did not at first appreciate the connection between the two. The job that I was doing in DHSS at the time required me to be a member of a particular committee which met regularly to decide on the future placement of individual delinquent children who were known to be particularly destructive or dangerous. The children themselves did not appear before the committee, and we had to make our decisions on the basis of case-notes and submissions, and these papers were a soul-searing amalgam of family neglect, angry despair, wanton destructiveness and inadequate responses by statutory authorities. One of my colleagues on the committee used to cope with all this by distancing himself from it; he devised a set of mechanistic criteria on which to base his recommendations, and his recommendations as a result were not usually very helpful. Another colleague, who felt all the pain that the case-notes conveyed, adopted the device of offloading it onto other people; I used to hear him making his way down the corridor invading everybody else's rooms so that he could tell them all about it and thus share his burden, and I used to be able to estimate to the minute the moment that he would invade mine. By the time he got to the end of the corridor he felt a great deal better and everybody else felt a great deal worse. And then there was an Executive Officer whose task it was to summarise the case-notes and prepare a digest to assist the committee. She used to perform this task very effectively, but in the course of doing it she used to absorb into herself all the suffering of the children and of their families and of their victims, and her manuscript draft, which I had to approve, used to arrive on my desk stained with the marks of her dried-up tears. Her capacity for perceiving all the names that appeared in the case-notes as living individuals was a great help in reminding the committee that it was deliberating the destinies of real people, and I found the knowledge of the pain she felt a great help to me in bearing mine. As I started committing to paper the confusion referred to earlier, I began to discover that my experience on this particular committee contained within itself some useful pointers to how a pattern within this confusion might be found.

As the pieces of paper began to pile up, it started to become clear that the difficulties that needed to be grappled with were not just those of reconciling being a DHSS civil servant with being an ordained priest; there was a much broader problem that needed to be addressed which was that of integrating the experience of paid employment within the framework of Christian belief. In the book that has resulted, the business of exercising an ordained ministry within the workplace has been relegated to a single chapter.

This book, then, is about the relationship between Christian belief and paid employment. It might be helpful, however, to spell out right at the start one or two things that it is not about. It is not about the relationship between Christian belief and the social problems surrounding paid employment, and in particular it is not about employment; I accept unemployment as evil in the sense that it denies people the opportunity for doing God's will by putting themselves effectively into practice, but this book offers no political, economic or even Christian suggestions as to how unemployment might be reduced or the problems that stem from it eased. Nor does it examine whether any particular political or economic standpoint, whether it be centrally planned socialism or unfettered capitalism or some point on the spectrum in between, is or is not compatible with the actualisation of the Kingdom; insofar as such a relationship is worth exploring I leave the task to others. And this book is only indirectly about the sort of work that people do outside the context of paid employment. I fully recognise that much if not most of the work that people do is not financially rewarded; being a householder, or being a parent, or looking after a handicapped or senile relative or friend, or even being an active member of the community involves a great deal of work that is often so demanding and so exhausting that if there were a trade union to represent people's interests in these capacities its strike calls would be almost continuous. The motivation for this sort of work it, however, somewhat different from the motivations that operate within paid employment, and the constraints that this sort of work imposes are different too. All that this book is about is what it is like to be a committed Christian and an employee.

I persevered with the task of collecting my pieces of paper into a bona fide book because of a growing awareness that such a book was urgently needed. My conclusions on the nature of this need in general terms are spelled out in the opening chapter, but there are two personal realisations that I would like to put on record here. The first was that my earlier attempts at expressing my Christian belief through the work that I was being paid to do started to seem naive and misguided; the writing of the book became, therefore, an exercise not just in exploration but in expiation. I started my working life as a schoolteacher and then became a lecturer in a teaching training college, and throughout these ten years I saw my concern for my students and my attempts to help them in their education as being a practical expression of my Christian beliefs. I then worked for a few years for a voluntary organisation which set up and managed community development projects in a number of deprived neighbourhoods throughout the country, and I saw my commitment to the people we were working with and to the social change we were attempting to bring about as being once again a manifestation of Christian witness, particularly since this social change envisaged a transfer of power and resources from the haves to the have-nots.

This straight forward relationship betwen work and belief started to seem less satisfactory when I made a major career change and joined the DHSS as a direct entry Principal in 1974. I saw the change at the time as a move from a position where I was only able to tinker with the system in a few of its isolated pockets to a position where I would be able to effect major alterations in the structure of society, but I quickly made two discoveries. The first was that what I was able to achieve as a civil servant was severely constrained by my obligation to implement the policies of the Government I was contracted to serve, and by the necessity of working through what are normally referred to as "the usual channels". The second was that social change was a very much more complex business than I had previously realised; I discovered that virtually every initiative had consequential implications, and indeed that most could be implemented only at the expense of desirable developments elsewhere. My early years as a civil servant were a painful period during which I had to learn to accept that my personal views about how the world ought to be, even if I expressed them in the terminology of the Kingdom, were of only marginal relevance, and that whereas there was some scope for my influencing the development of policy and the manner of its implementation within my own minute area or responsibility, this had to happen from within the system if it were to happen at all; for the most part my task was merely to keep my own little bit of the system operating smoothly. This required a rethink of the Christian connection.

And my second realisation arose from my experience as a student on the Southwark Ordination Course, which I embarked upon and completed while working full-time as a civil servant. Of the twenty-one ordinands in my year group, two were ful-time mothers and the other nineteen were in full-time employment doing a wide range of jobs and intending to remain in them after ordination. I enjoyed the course, and felt it to be a good preparation for ministry, but one aspect that disappointed me greatly was that very little thinking seemed to have been done at the interface between paid employment and Christian belief and witness. This vacuum mattered for the members of my year group since it left them without a framework for relating their ministry and secular work, and it continues to matter, not only for subsequent generation of ordinands in paid employment, but for all Christians who are employees.

I need to express my gratitude to a number of people whose situations and predicaments have stimulated the thinking which has gone into this book, in particular to my colleagues in the civil service and my fellow students on the Southwark Ordination Course, and also the clergy and congregations of three churches, St James the Less in Pimlico, and St Matthews and Crossway United Reform Church which are on opposite sides of the New Kent Road a few yards away from the DHSS headquarters at the Elephant and Castle. I am also grateful to a smaller number of people, some of whose names are listed in the acknowledgements, who read the manuscript at one or more of its various stages and made comments of varying degrees of ferocity.

One outcome of this consultation was that a fellow priest-worker who is a barrister and therefore self-employed pointed out that I had made the assumption that all remunerated work is done by the employees of employing institutions. His analysis is correct, and I therefore apologise to people reading this book who are either in business on their own account or earn their living by receiving fees, but I hope the principles expounded are applicable to their predicaments with only minor modifications.

A second criticism, from a deaconess, upset me a great deal more. She accused me of sexism, and though in no way would I wish to promulgate a sexist attitude I have to admit that her charge has some foundation. To some extent these failings are not so much my fault as the inevitable result of the difficulties inherent on our linguistic traditions. I had to decide, therefore, to retain phrases like the "Doctrine of Man" which people know about rather than to talk about a "Doctrine of Humanity" which people might have thought was something new. And for the time being there is no way round the problems that result from the use of the masculine pronoun either when referring to hypothetical individuals or when referring to God; when a new terminology is developed I will be among the first to make use of it. However the charge runs deeper than this and I am aware that the vast majority of the examples I use are to do with men. This is partly because the centuries old demarcation between women staying at home while men go out to work has only been partially eroded; I am very aware that many of the women who stay at home work harder than their husbands who go off to their jobs, but then this book is about paid employment rather than work in general. And partly it is because in identifying with people in paid employment I suppose I have identified more readily with men that with women; insofar as this may have distorted my perspective, I can only apologise and ask readers to make their own adjustments.

When I started telling people that I had embarked upon a book about the relationship between paid employment and Christian belief, a number told me that the task would be impossible because everybody's workplace predicaments were so different. I was never deterred by this warning since my objective was to identify the highest common factor of paid employment, those aspects of workplace experience that are shared by all employees. For this reason I have made the illustrative examples deliberately generalised, and in particular I have tried hard to restrict examples drawn from the civil service; this is partly because being a civil servant is not a very typical job (but then what is?), and partly it is because I did not wish to run the risk of falling foul of the Official Secrets Act. The illustrations drawn from teaching are based on first hand experience, and those drawn from medicine, nursing, social work, social security, the judiciary, the police and the prison service are based on second hand experience gained through my DHSS work. The references to farming have some authenticity since I was brought up in a farming community, but the references to the making and selling of washing machines are totally hypothetical, which is a pity; my experience of industry and commerce is very limited and I can only hope that this doesn't show too badly or matter too much. There are also a number of references to the hunting of mammoths in an attempt to create the illusion of an anthropological perspective.

I hope that this book is helpful to people in paid employment, both to those who have struggled with the difficulties inherent in reconciling Christian and contractual obligations, and to those who have never bothered to think about them. In this sense it is written prayerfully. It is also written in humility, since I am by no means certain that I have got it right. I am, however, certain that there is a vacuum that needs to be filled, and I would be only too happy if someone else were to fill it more ably than I.

Acknowledgements

I would like to thank a number of people who have read and commented on the manuscript of this book at one or more stages of development and made helpful comments, including Andrew Henderson, Keith Holt, Eric James, Janet Lewis Jones, James Mark, Paul Nicholson, Michael Ranken, Jill Robson, Malcolm Torry, Patrick Vaughan, Anthony Winter, Pat Winterton and my brother Jeremy and sister-in-law Elizabeth. And I would particularly like to thank Christopher Martin, Graham Morgan, John Sherriff and my wife Vicky for their more sustained and extensive assistance and support.

Some, but not all, of the quotations used in the historical survey of Christian attitudes to work in the middle of the first chapter are taken from a very helpful package on *Work* produced by the General Synod for Social Responsibility Industrial Committee in 1979; I would like to express my gratitude to its anonymous compilers and commend the package to others.

And finally, since I am a civil servant, I am obliged to make it clear that the views expressed in this book are mine alone and that its contents in no way commit either Government or the Department of Health and Social Security.

An Allegory

Once upon a time in the days before anybody took children very seriously, there was an enlightened local authority superintendant of parks. This superintendant thought it would be nice to do something for the children, so he started making the necessary plans and preparations. He decided that what would suit the children best would be a large adventure playground, and he set about creating one. He brought in the bulldozers and made some mountains, and he planted trees on the mountains, and he imported squirrels to run up the trees, and he saw that it was all pretty good. And then he let the children in.

Being a good developmental psychologist, he appreciated that what the children would need if they were to grow and mature into the sort of healthy adults who would thrive in the big wide world beyond the adventure playground would be plenty of space and plenty of opportunity for unsupervised creative play. So he ensured that the playground included sufficient scope for everybody to do whatever suited him or her best, with complex pieces of apparatus on which they could test their skills and little shelters in which they could play house. But inevitably, because children are children, they sometimes fought each other over who should have the next go on a particular piece of apparatus, and some of them were capable of setting fire to the apparatus or taking an axe to it just for the hell of it, and even some of the best designed pieces of apparatus were capable of being the scene of one or two nasty accidents.

He was very sad whenever he saw things going wrong, and particularly whenever he saw children encouraging others in getting it wrong, and even more so whenever he saw children vandalising the equipment so that the scope for other children to get it right was reduced; he was sad chiefly because he appreciated that if the children got it wrong in the adventure playground it would mean that it would be that much harder for them to be successful as the adults they were destined to become. But nevertheless he maintained the hope that some day everybody would get it right simultaneously, and then the adventure playground would in every sense have justified itself. And yet he realised that there was an important sense in which the adventure playground had already justified itself since the scope for everybody to get it right had been built into the playground from the beginning, since that was the way in which it had been planned; this was borne out by the extent to which some of the children did get it right some of the time.

After some time the superintendant, watching the children in the playground, started to worry about the extent to which they were failing to appreciate the magnificent opportunities that the playground offered and didn't realise what the playground was actually for. He came to the conclusion that the only way that he could explain it all would be to go into the playground himself, but he didn't want to do this because the presence of an adult would upset the whole balance of the activities that were going on, and in any event it was for children that the playground had been created. But he had a son who knew just as much about the purpose of the playground as his father because he had heard his father talking about it and had actually helped in the planning. So father and son agreed that the son would go into the playground in order to demonstrate the purpose of the playground and how to get the best out of it.

The son realised that this would be difficult since the children were too little to appreciate the jargon of developmental psychology, and that he would have to use only words which the children were able to understand. And, of course, he realised from the outset that there were too many children in the playground for him to be able to speak to all of them, so he had to hope that the children who heard him would pass the message on to others. But what he found was that most of the children just couldn't understand the message however simply he expressed it, chiefly because they were so intent on playing their own games; indeed some of them felt very threatened because what he was talking about seemed to them to undermine the importance of the games that they had developed and which they enjoyed playing. Some of these children were used to playing games that involved bashing other children, and unsurprisingly they bashed the superintendant's son; worse than that, they actually killed him. But his death didn't negate the purpose of the playground; indeed the fact that the purpose of the playground was unaffected by such an awful event helped a number of children to appreciate what a wonderful resource the playground was, and the fact that the children who had been involved in his death weren't punished or expelled made it somehow easier for them to profit from the opportunities on offer.

A number of the children who had actually met the superintendant's son did manage to understand something of what he had been saying about what the playground was for and how they could most profit from it. This had the effect on them both of making them want to profit from it as much as possible themselves, and also of making them want to tell as many other children as possible how they could profit from it too. During the son's lifetime this was comparatively straightforward because all they had to do was listen to him and encourage others to listen to him, but after his death the task became more difficult because he was no longer around in person. Nevertheless they were determined to continue, but they found that they could only do it if they reminded themselves continually of what it was that he had shown them, and of how even the brutality of his killing hadn't altered or diminished the playground's purpose. So what they did was to continue playing a particular game which he himself had taught them, using as much as possible his actual words, and this reminded them both of what he had said and of what had happened; indeed this game was so effective that they were actually able to be him during the reenactment of the events. Because this aspect of the game was so important and needed to be taken so seriously, it was decided that it should only be played when it was presided over by somebody who was especially committed to it and who understood properly what it was about; these children became special in this particular respect, but that didn't stop them from being children in every other respect the same as everybody else.

As time went on, special pieces of apparatus came to be developed which were no different from all the other pieces of apparatus except in three particular and not very important respects. First, they required a particular type of concentration if the children were to get the best out of playing on them. This meant that there was little scope for the children to stand back and admire the playground as a whole, or wonder what it was all for, or think about what other pieces of apparatus to try next; all this had to wait until the children got off the apparatus at the end of the day. Second, they required behaviour in accordance with certain rules, especially in relation to cooperation with other children who were playing on the apparatus at the same time. This meant that they were not able to behave or relate to each other except in the way that the apparatus dictated; if they wanted to do something different, this also had to wait until they got off. And third, once the children had started, they had to go back to the same apparatus day after day; this meant that it might become a bit monotonous and that the children might hanker after other experiences or even fail to appreciate what other opportunities there were, but it did have the advantage that they got to know a particular piece of apparatus really well and were thus well placed to get the most out of it. It also meant that they were likely to be well occupied and unlikely to spend their time moping around doing nothing.

Inevitably some of the children who knew about the superintendant's son, including some who had been chosen to preside over the reenactment of what he had said, found themselves playing on the special apparatus, even though this meant that while they were there they had to spend most of their time concentrating on the apparatus instead of musing on the playground's broader purpose. Nevertheless the superintendant was quite glad to see them there because it meant that these particular children were able to play with all the other children on the special apparatus and to share in their games, and also because it meant that they were able to come back at the end of the day and tell other children who remembered his son what playing on the special apparatus was like. There hadn't been very much of this special apparatus around at the time when the superintendant's son had been killed, so what he had said and done hadn't taken the special apparatus very much into account, so it was useful for these new experiences to be incorporated into the more important aspects of his message.

1

Two Worlds:
The Need for a Framework for Integration

This book is concerned with establishing a framework within which two facts, not often thought of in association with each other, can be reconciled and related. The first, though some people would call it an assumption rather than a fact, is that being aware of being loved by God gives people a true sense of their own identity, an enhanced appreciation of the created world and the people who live in it, and a structure within which attitudes, motivations and relationships can be made sense of and can develop. The second, which is an indisputable fact, is that nowadays most people, including most committed Christians, spend not far short of half their waking lives outside the home in paid employment.

I am constantly saddened by how few of the Christians I meet and talk with have ever thought of applying the insights that stem from their awareness of God's love and their belief in the divinity of Jesus to the world of their workplaces. They seem to see their Christian beliefs as being relevant to their lives at home and in their home communities but not to their lives at work and in their work communities, and as a result they have forfeited important opportunities for increasing their understanding of God and of his world, for furthering God's will, and for worship and prayer. I am equally saddened by how few of the people I meet at work, who seem to have a proper sense of their own value as individuals which can only have its origin in God's love, and who live their lives on the responsible assumption that all people and all things deserve a proper respect which can only have its origin in God's will, have ever thought of looking to Christianity as a foundation in which such attitudes might be grounded. In the absence of any such framework there is no means by which any dialogue between the experience of Christian belief and the experience of paid employment can be developed, whether it be within an individual person, or within a particular community, or in general terms that are capable of particular application. It is as though there were two separate worlds, and nobody seems to be bothering about how they might be integrated or what the implications of such integration might be.

This separateness has been reinforced by tradition, not so much by tradition going back to Biblical times, as by tradition going back some two hundred years or so since most people stopped working in or close to their own homes. Within this tradition, parochial clergy have tended to define their parishioners as being those people who live in their parishes and not those who work in them, churchgoing has traditionally been associated with Sundays when most workplaces are closed, and the main focus of pastoral care has been on people in their homes rather than on people in their workplaces. Perhaps also people have tended to see their home lives as being their main source of joy, of suffering, and of personal growth, while they have seen work as being essentially mechanistic and thus beyond religion's remit. And perhaps also this tradition has become self-perpetuating in that the Church has failed to develop a whole area of experience and expertise with the result that, even when opportunities for involvement in the world of paid employment have been offered, it has been unable to capitalise on them.

But the separateness is not just to do with this tradition. There are also a number of very real difficulties which have to be faced, analysed, and resolved before any framework which integrates paid employment and Christian belief can be successful in practice. Perhaps what underlies these difficulties is that the currency of Christian witness is love whereas the currency of paid employment is money, and love and money operate in accordance with different sets of rules. The basis of the difference is that, whereas money is a finite resource, love is an infinite resource. Every housewife and every health authority chairman knows that the amount of money available to be spent is limited, and that you can only spend more money on one thing if you spend less money on something else. There is always, of course, the possibility of the amount of money available being increased in some way, and though this might initially make the allocation process somewhat easier, what inevitably tends to happen is that expectations rise so that there still isn't enough money to give everybody everything they would like. Even people who are in the business of making money, buying things

2

at one price and selling them at a somewhat higher price, whether they be shopkeepers or stockbrokers, will appreciate that the price they can sell at is constrained by the finite amount of money that potential buyers have available to spend, and this constraint applies all the way to the beginning of the chain, to farmers who want to sell beans that have grown up out of the earth and to potters who have made pots from mud scooped up from the river bed.

Love, on the other hand, is an infinite resource. Even an agnostic would agree that somebody who loves another person deeply and genuinely is better able and not less to love other people as a result; love for a third person does not mean love taken away from the second but more love all round. And God's love is absolutely infinite. When we talk about everybody being paid an equal wage, the implication is that what everybody would receive would be an average wage which in turn would imply that some people have to receive less. However when we say that everybody is equal in God's love, we don't mean that God loves each person an average amount, we mean that he loves each person totally, and insofar as people are unequally aware of being loved by God it is because of variations in their individual receptivity.

The fact that the two currencies operate in accordance with different rules means that dealing in money and dealing in love have to happen in accordance with different criteria. The first criterion in the allocation of money is fairness; each person should have the share they deserve and no more since anything else would mean some people getting less than they deserve. The second criterion is efficiency; money should be spent on what is most important since anything else would mean that it was frittered away on inessentials. And the third criterion is cost-effectiveness: money should be invested where it will yield the most beneficial return since anything else would be wasteful. In the money world fairness, efficiency and cost-effectiveness are virtues, but in the love world they are evil constraints. Love is available to all for the asking so what matters is being prepared to respond to demand, and the criterion for this is generosity; if love were allocated fairly it would mean that the well-loved would have to be denied it. Love is available to all who need it so what matters is being prepared to identify need, and the criterion

3

for this is compassion; if love were allocated efficiently it would mean that it would have to be denied to people who were somehow defined as less important. Love is available irrespective of it being offered in return so what matters is being prepared to bear the pain of rejection, and the criterion is a willingness to be vulnerable; if love were allocated only where benefits were likely to accure it would have to be denied to those who did not know how to offer love in response. Generosity, compassion and a willingness to be vulnerable are virtues in the love world, but the problem is that any business managed by people in whom these virtues were the primary motivation would soon be in the hands of the official receiver.

This difference between the finite and the infinite underlies a number of specific difficulties that individual employees are likely to experience in reconciling their paid employment with their Christian belief. The first is to do with the obligations that an employer imposes on an employee as the conditions of his contract of employment; an employee is obliged to act in pursuit of his employer's objectives irrespective of whether or not this is compatible with, let alone a positive expression of, his vision of the Kingdom of God. This difficulty is often compounded by a feeling of powerlessness. The majority of employees feel themselves to be small cogs in large machines, while Christianity lays a special emphasis on the value of each individual and on his personal responsibility for his actions; how can an employee exercise Christian witness or exert Christian influence from a small cog position? The second difficulty is to do with values. While at work, an employee is expected to pursue his employer's objectives singlemindedly, and often assertively and even aggressively; how can this be reconciled with the values traditionally associated with Christianity which are based upon selflessness and sacrificial love? And money is not the only finite resource, time is another, and this gives rise to a third difficulty. When a person is at work, he has a number of specific tasks to perform which are defined with varying degrees of precision by his employer; if he is under a contractual obligation to get these tasks done, how can he make himself available to respond to any demands that God may choose to make on him during working hours? And since most paid employment happens in institutions that are hierarchical, these difficulties are compounded for

4

people who are in postions to managerial responsibility; for a person to resolve his own set of dilemmas is hard enough, but for a manager to require that other people solve their sets of dilemmas in ways that ensure that the interests of the institution are properly safeguarded is even harder.

It has to be admitted that it is difficult to find within the pages of the New Testament any direct guidance on how these problems might be resolved. In St Matthew's Sermon on the Mount, people are exhorted to walk a second mile when they are asked to walk one, and this is not very helpful advice to an employee wondering how he should best spend his time. People are also exhorted to give their coats also when asked for their shirts, and this is hardly helpful guidance to an employee who is looking for ground-rules on how scarce resources might best be allocated between competing priorities. In the same chapter 6 of St Matthew and again in chapter 13 of St Luke, Jesus actually says "You cannot serve God and Mammon", and it is difficult not to take this as implying that being a genuine Christian and being in paid employment are somehow mutually exclusive, at any rate where being in paid employment includes some trace of an obligation to strive towards cost-effectiveness or the optimisation of profits. The passage in St Matthew chapter 22 from which this book takes its title implies that one set of things are appropriate for rendering unto God while a totally different set of things, which presumably would include most of the things associated with paid employment, are appropriate for rendering unto Caesar, with no apparent area of overlap. And the parable of the labourers in the vineyard in St Matthew chapter 20 is either about real money, in which case any personnel manager worth his salt would reject it as a crazy basis for an industrial relations strategy, or it is using money as a metaphor for love, in which case the point Jesus is making is the one about finite and infinite resources; it would certainly have been important for Jesus to have made this point about the infinite nature of love to a commercially minded world, but the difficulty is that he didn't follow it up by offering any guidance to people motivated by love on how to reconcile this with running a commercially successful vineyard.

Against this sort of background, it is not surprising that a large number of Christian employees have opted for a simple solution which is to split their lives in two, to apply their Christian beliefs to their home lives and to their personal relationships and to conduct their work lives in accordance with an entirely different set of criteria. This is a tempting solution, and in many ways a viable one; the ethos that exists within most workplaces is an acceptable one in the sense that for the most part it is not manifestly incompatible with Christian values, and if a person leaves behind at home any obligation he might feel to be generous, compassionate or vulnerable he can at least concentrate on getting the work done. However the assumption that underlies this book is that this splitting in two is an inadequate solution; it creates a stumbling block for honest agnostics who take their work seriously but might be prepared to consider Christianity in their search for a more all-embracing framework, while for Christians it fails to recognise the full dimension of God's care and concern and denies them a whole spectrum of opportunities for wonder, for worship, for witness, for prayer and for loving.

In seeking an adequate solution, there is little help to be gained from examining how the relationship between Christian commitment and paid employment has been dealt with in the past, largely no doubt because previous generations have perceived and defined the problems differently from the way that we perceive and define them today. The mediaeval solution, as encapsulated by St Thomas Aquinas, was to see religious activity as being more acceptable to God than economic activity; he saw work as being by its nature something rather second class, at best a step on the way to higher things and at worst a distraction from the more important business of prayer and worship. This solution is not a very helpful one nowadays, since only a very disgruntled employee would agree to the importance of his paid employment being downgraded in this way. The solution offered by Martin Luther centred on a single word in Ecclesiasticus chapter 11 verse 21, which reads in the Authorised Version: "Trust in the Lord and abide in thy labour". The New English Bible uses the word "job", and Luther used the word "Beruf" which literally means vocation or calling. Luther saw everyone as being called by God to his particular vocation, whether it be to be a carpenter or a silversmith or a full time religious, and he saw the pursuit of ths vocation as the

6

performance of God's will and its end product as an expression of worship. The concept of vocation is helpful to some people nowadays particularly in the caring professions, but when it is applied to industrial work it assumes something of a William Morris aura and conjures up pictures of an artist craftsman; it is difficult to apply to employment within a large institution where the scope for individual creativity is constrained by a hierarchical structure and where freedom of action is constrained by job descriptions and terms and conditions of service. John Calvin, in contrast, had a simple solution which was to do away with the problem; for him what mattered was whether or not a person had been saved in the first place, and if this person were fortunate enough to be thus one of the elect anything he might do during working hours would be by definition acceptable to God. Calvin indeed went further and linked the Reformation virtue of hard work with the Mediaeval virtue of obedience, and under his influence first Geneva and later Edinburgh became thriving centres of commerce, underpinned by great personal self-confidence and inhibited only by the sort of scruple that was manifestly good for business. Most people nowadays retain something of a Calvinistic attitude towards their work but have abandoned his religious perspective; restoring the religious perspective, though not in an altogether Calvanistic form, is what this book is about.

Thinking within the reformed tradition in England was dominated by a particular dilemma; on the one hand hard work was considered virtuous, but on the other hand hard work was likely to generate increased wealth and this was likely to be dangerous since it would inevitably lead first to temptation and then to corruption. The solution to the dilemma offered by Martin Bucer, a contemporary of Luther and like him a German, but professor of divinity at Cambridge, was that the only people who should be allowed to engage in trade would be those who put benefitting the commonwealth ahead of benefitting themselves; it is difficult to see this viewpoint as opening the way for anything except Pharisaic hypocrisy. Richard Baxter, a contemporary of Cromwell, offered a neat solution which has ever since been a stock-in-trade for all theocratic dictatorships including Marxist ones; he said that people should be encouraged to work hard since this was good for them, but that they should not be allowed to keep any of the wealth they generated since this might be bad for them. Even John Wesley was foxed by this dilemma; he said in the course of a single sermon both "I fear that whenever riches have increased the essence of religion has decreased in the same proportion", and "We ought not to prevent people from being diligent and frugal; we must exhort all Christians to gain all they can and save all they can, that is, in effect, to grow rich". His solution was that people should indeed be encouraged to work hard and to generate wealth, but that they should then give away all the wealth they generated in charitable donations. It is remarkable how many of the early Methodists did exactly this, though these tended to be employers rather than employees.

Roman Catholic thinking during the last hundred years, interestingly and in contrast, has been focussed almost entirely on the shop floor, and the four encyclicals about work, those of 1891, 1931, 1961 and 1981, have all had remarkably little to say about what it is like to be anywhere other than at the bottom of an institutional hierarchy. All these encyclicals attempted to come to terms with a somewhat different dilemma; they were anxious to demonstrate concern for the degrading exploitation of shop floor workers while at the same time making it clear that the socialist solution was unacceptable. Pope Leo XIII in 1891 preached acceptance, and he linked industrial exploitation with original sin in the terrifying words: "As regards bodily labour, even had man never fallen from the state of innocence, he would not have remained wholly unoccupied; but that which would then have been his free choice and his delight, became afterwards compulsory and the painful expiation of his disobedience. To suffer and to endure, therefore, is the lot of humanity".

Forty years later Pope Pius XI introduced the concept of human dignity in the workplace, and pleaded that it be properly respected in a particularly striking image: "And so bodily labour, which even after the original sin was decreed by Providence for the good of man's body and soul, is in many instances changed into an instrument of perversion; for from the factory dead matter goes our improved, whereas men there are corrupted and degraded". He suggested cooperation within the workplace as the means whereby this respect might be achieved:

8

"Unless intelligence, capital and labour combine together for common effort, man's toil cannot produce adequate fruit". The two most recent encyclicals, those of Pope John XXIII and Pope John Paul II, both saw work as a means of personal self-fulfilment: "That a man should develop and perfect himself through his daily work, which is in most cases of a temporal character, is perfectly in keeping with the plan of divine Providence". This is one of the concepts developed during the course of this book, but neither encyclical offers any guidance on how conflicts between temporal and divine requirements might be resolved.

The Lambeth Conference Report of 1897 avoided Pope Leo XIII's demarcation between employers and workers and saw work as "the honourable task and privilege of all", but it drew an equally terrifying demarcation between the employed and the unemployed whom it saw as " the unfit, the unfortunate, and the morally weak". A report of the Archbishops' Committee of Enquiry in 1918 attempted to solve the problems inherent in relating Christianity and paid employment by saying that there shouldn't be any: "It is the duty of the Church, while avoiding dogmatism as to the precise methods of applying Christian principles to industry, to insist that Christian ethics are as binding upon economic conduct and industrial organisation as upon personal conduct and domestic life. By so doing, it would modify the assumptions which men bring into the transactions of economic life, and would cause them to judge industry and industrial success by moral and not merely by economic criteria". If it were this straightforward, there would have been no need to have written this book! Archbishop Temple, in expounding his "social gospel", said many sensible things about industrial organisation and certainly reversed the earlier attitude towards the unemployed, but added little to the resolution of this particular difficulty: "Economic enterprise in a Christian community should be seen as a three-fold relationship; first, management aiming to give every worker the opportunity for soul-satisfying creative work, secondly the worker doing the best work of which he is capable, as a creative activity and in a spirit of service to the community, and thirdly each individual worker recognising that he can only express himself and play his part fully in brotherly comradeship with his fellow workers". There is very little about how the enterprise should reconcile all this with making a profit. More recent thinking both within the Anglican Church and within the World Council of Churches has been preoccupied with the societal structure within which work takes place and with the effect of work upon the earth and its resources; so little has been said about what it is actually like to be employed that it seems as though no one with experience of paid employment within a secular institution has ever been consulted. It now seems that there are two things wrong with paid employment; one is that it leads to a materialistic attitude and despoils the earth, and the other is that such opportunities for materialism and despoiling are denied to too many people.

In the absence of any helpful guidance, it is not surprising that some of the individual people who have attempted to relate their Christian belief to their paid employment experience have got the nature of that relationship somewhat wrong; as well as the temptation to place Christianity and paid employment in separate boxes, there is also the temptation to take elements of the one and equate them inappropriately with elements of the other. How this can happen may be illustrated by four actual examples. The first concerns a young man who left university with a proven expertise in computer programming and a first class degree in mathematics. During his time as an undergraduate he had developed a strong commitment to Christianity, but had somehow come to accept the view that computer programming was not a very Christian activity and that the most appropriate career for a committed Christian was some form of social work. So he became a probation officer. He was not very good at it because he was the sort of person who was not very good at forming relationships with people who held cultural assumptions very different from his own, and he became very frustrated. What happened next was that he rejected his Christian beliefs, and this enable him to leave the probation service and become a paid computer programmer. The story has a happy ending in that he prospered in computers, and then returned to Church membership.

The second example concerns a farm manager who ran his farm very effectively at the same time as being a stalwart member of his village church. Then his wife developed chronic kidney failure and became very ill. She spent about three years on haemodialysis in their home and then received a kidney transplant and became very much better. During this period the husband's assumptions underwent a radical change; first he had to take on board the very real possibility that his wife might die, and then he had to devote a great deal of time and effort both to helping his wife with her dialysis and to looking after the children. This resulted in an enormous deepening of his Christian faith, and gave him a new insight into the meaning of service which enabled him to support his family during this very difficult period. However he also started to apply these same beliefs to the management of the farm but the result was that his deliberate kindness and his concern to "serve" his workers were interpreted as weakness and his authority as a manager collapsed; standards of performance deteriorated and the farm slipped from profit into loss. The landlord, who had inherited the farm but never worked on it and had no farming expertise, trusted the manager completely and was totally dependant on him; he was unable to take action and unwilling to dismiss the manager and justified this in terms of Christian charity. This story has a less happy ending in that the farm had to be sold and the manager and his family had to leave the village so that he could start a new career as a salesman for agricultural equipment.

The third example concerns a young man who was advised by the Advisory Council on the Church's Ministry to spend some time working on a shop floor before starting full time ordination training. He duly started work in a factory but only a few days later he was dismissed; it transpired that from his very first day he had embarked upon an earnest programme of evangelism which had so enraged his shop floor colleagues that they had conspired to make life impossible for him and to have him removed. He explained all this to his Diocesan Director of Ordinands by saying that the entire management and staff of the factory were deaf to the word of the Lord, and he asked if he might be allowed to work in a more Christian environment. What happened after this incident I don't know, but I suspect that the Church of England decided in its wisdom that he was fit only for ordination.

And finally there was a Scale II secondary school teacher in London who applied for a head of department post in a school in

West Yorkshire. He was shortlisted and went for an interview, but was then turned down. He came back from Yorkshire exhibiting no outward signs of anger or disappointment, and he interpreted the decision of the selection committee as the way in which God's will was made known, convincing himself that this meant that God wished him to remain a Scale II teacher in London. The last time I saw him, which was several years after the interview, he was still in his original job.

All societies and all religions have recognised man's special capacities for working and for loving. In the world of paid employment primacy is given to work but Jesus, both in his teaching and by his example, stressed the primacy of love. Most of the problems that need to be faced in the integration of paid employment and Christian belief within a single framework stem from the difficulties inherent in the reconciliation of these different priorities. Perhaps the difficulties that the four people in these examples got themselves into resulted from their attempting this integration at too early a stage before the world of work's essential characteristics had been properly clarified and understood. What went wrong for the computer programmer stemmed not from his desire to reflect God's love, but from his mistaken definition of being a probation officer as a better form of loving than programming computers; both are, in fact, different forms of work. Loving is the reflection of God's infinite sympathy and concern which continues whatever human shortcomings may occur to distract it, where as work is defining a number of necessary tasks and seeing that they get done; the difficulty that the farm manager got himself into resulted from his desire to reflect God's concern and forgiveness in a context where the effective performance of his managerial tasks might more appropriately have been accorded priority. Workplace communities exist in order to get work done and are committed to work-based values; the young man on the shop floor felt an obligation to proclaim the good news of the Gospel in a context where the effect of the good news was to disrupt the work and was not what his colleagure wanted to hear at the time. Loving God means being aware of his presence in all things, whereas getting work done requires having an eye to defined objectives; what the schoolteacher did was to confuse the selection committee's obligation to perform its proper task of choosing the best man for a particular job with such obligations its individual members may have felt to implement God's will. Staying at the school in London may well have been God's will for him, but the fact that a selection committee in Yorkshire decided that someone else would be a better head of department was not in itself evidence that this was so.

The purpose of this book is to suggest a framework within which the experiences of paid employment and the experiences of Christian commitment can be integrated to the enhancement of both, and in attempting this it adopts a very deliberate structure. The chapter that follows lays the foundations for this framework by identifying the common origin of both sets of experiences; it looks at man in the context of God's creation and at work in the context of the nature of man. The four chapters after that examine in greater detail the essential characteristics of paid employment in order to demonstrate the differences between the obligations an employee is bound by in entering into a contract of employment and the obligations, if that is the right word, that stem from an awareness of God's love; a framework for integration will not be viable unless it is based on a full and realistic appreciation of what paid employment actually entails. Chapters 7, 8 and 9 fill out the framework by looking at the position within paid employment of the individual, the ordained ministry and the Church, and they examine a number of particular difficulties and more generally the scope that exists within the workplace for the glorification of God. In the final chapter paid employment takes its place as just one of the ingredients, albeit an increasingly important one, of the Kingdom of God.

2

The Common Ground: Creation, Man and Work

It is not the intention of this book to examine in detail the doctrine of creation or the doctrine of the nature of man, but work cannot be looked at in isolation from the nature of man, and the nature of man cannot be looked at in isolation from creation. The purpose of this chapter is to establish the common ground within which both Christian belief and paid employment have their origins, and to provide a starting point for the examination of the relationship between them.

The story of creation in the first chapter of Genesis has a special place in any examination of paid employment since it might almost be described as the story of the first working week, and like most working weeks it starts in chaos and ends with a well-earned day off. The story shows God's creative task as being the transformation of this chaos into order, and during the first five days of creation he orders the world and everything in it. This ordering is an act of love since it provides every created thing with the opportunity for putting itself into practice and thus for doing God's will. Mountains can be mountains and incidentally provide somewhere for trees to grow, trees can be trees and incidentally proved a habitat for squirrels, and squirrels can be squirrels. If there had been no creation not only would there have been no squirrels but also there would have been no opportunity for squirrels to do squirrelish things, so the most loving act possible for squirrels was first to create them and then to create a world that includes trees for them to climb up and nuts for them to eat.

But there is one part of creation that is different from all the others and that is man. When God creates man on the sixth day of creation, he gives him a very specific charge which is that he should cultivate the earth and make it fruitful. And when God rests from his labours on the seventh day of creation because he has completed what he had set himself to do, there is a clear implication that he delegates to man the responsibility for the continuation of the creative task, for transforming chaos into order and for cultivating the earth and making it fruitful. The reason why man is capable of exercising this responsibility is because of the unique gift of free will. Man is similar to the rest of the animal part of creation in the sense that human beings are born, need to eat, and eventually die, but different in that part of God's will for him is that he should exercise a will of his own. Looked at anthropologically, there must have been a moment in time when man first discovered that he had the capacity to decide what he would do next, in contrast to squirrels who do not have and never have had the capacity to choose to do anything other than carry on squirreling.

But like most blessings the gift of free will is double-edged. Since a squirrel does not have the capacity for choice, there is no alternative to squirreling available to it, so it cannot do anything other than express God's will for squirrels all the time. That is not to say that things never go wrong in the parts of creation where man's influence is unfelt; part of God's gift to squirrels includes owls to keep them on their toes. The fact that the world is inhabited by an infinite number of very different created things means that there are inevitably instances where one part of creation can only put itself into practice at the expense of another part. In eating nuts squirrels kill off a number of potential trees and owls by their nature kill off a number of squirrels. This destruction is an intrinsic part of God's will being done, even when the destruction is catastrophic as when rivers flood or volcanoes erupt, and even when whole species disappear as happened with dinosaurs and dodos. God's will has an eternal perspective which means that what happened once and is not happening any more does not lose its significance. God's love as expressed by a squirrel squirreling one moment is not negated by the disappearance of the squirrel as the result of an owl owling the next. Man, on the other hand, by virtue of his capacity for choice, is able to do things that are not the inbuilt instinctual responses of a human being to the situations he is placed in, and this means that he is capable of choosing to do things that are other than God's will for human beings. And yet it is God's will for him that he should have this capacity for choice even though the inevitable result is that the opposite of God's will is sometimes done. This aspect of that anthropological moment is vividly encapsulated in the third chapter of Genesis when Adam and Eve eat the apple from the tree of knowledge of good and evil; they exercise their God-given freedom to make their own decisions which inevitably includes the disobeying of God's will.

This capacity for choice is the expression of God's special love for man because uniquely among species God's love for man includes trust. God has to trust man to do his will and man is capable of living up to this trust only some of the time. Man's failure in this trust occurs whenever an individual human being exercises his capacity to choose and makes a divergent decision. However failure in trust also occurs because humanity is by now so far removed in time from that anthropological moment when the capacity to choose was first realised that it is no longer crystal clear in every instance what God's will for human beings actually is; the human equivalent of running up trees and eating nuts is only very rarely an option. Life has become very much more complicated than it ever was in the Garden of Eden, and the cumulative divergent decisions of so many generations of humanity have created a cultural climate in which learning from the examples proffered by other people does not mean that what we learn is necessarily synonymous with God's will. Because of this lack of clarity some divine help is necessary, and one of the purposes of the incarnation is that people should have before them in the human form of Jesus an example of what God's will for human beings actually is. There has never been any need for God to be incarnated as a squirrel because God's will for squirrels is abundantly clear and apparent wherever there are squirrels.

Another of the purposes of the incarnation is to do with demonstrating that God's love for individual people is capable of continuing through the most awful predicaments that people are capable of experiencing. The destructive effects that sometimes follow from human beings diverging from God's will are such that sometimes it does not appear conceivable that God has any concern for humanity at all, either for those who suffer from the damage or for those who perpetrate it. What was done to Jesus on the cross was at least as awful as anything that can be imagined happening to anybody, and the fact that it was followed by the resurrection is proof that God's concern continues.

17

Man's capacity for choosing not to do God's will makes man unique among creation and is evidence that man is the object of God's special love. Most of what is important about the nature of man follows from this, and there are five aspects of this uniqueness that are particularly relevant. The first is that man is unique in his capacity to know God. Consequent upon man's capability for doing what is not God's will is his ability to appreciate the difference between what is not God's will and what is, and this is the origin of man's unique understanding, however partial, of what God's will actually is; at the very least it means that man is capable of realising that God is actually there. In the same way that an ability to discern darkness is necessary for an appreciation of light so man, in consequence of his ability to discern the capacity of his species to deny the purpose of creation, is capable of appreciating what that purpose is. Knowledge of God is implied by a perception of the immensity of this purpose and by the need to wonder at it.

The second aspect of man's uniqueness is his capacity to love. A perception of the purpose in the world implies an awareness of the extent to which the world is loved, and an awareness of being specially loved as part of it. This awareness cannot but result in the reflection of that love towards everybody and everything, and the expression of that love in action. Of course the gift of free will means that man is capable of choosing both to close himself off from this love and not to express it in action, and being at the tail-end of generations who have had the capacity to choose to deny it means that being blind to it is sometimes the norm. Each person has to rediscover this love for himself, but the scope for doing so is indubitably there. And the fact that man is capable of loving is tantamount to saying that man has a need to love.

The third of man's unique capacities is his capacity to suffer. Man shares with animals and with other parts of creation the capacity for experiencing physical pain, but suffering is something beyond this. It stems from an awareness, or at least a suspicion, that things are not as they ought to be, and this implied capacity for an awareness of how things ought to be is again consequential upon his capacity for choice. At one level this awareness is idiosyncratic in the sense that the perception of how things ought to be is peculiar to the person concerned; this

18

includes, but is certainly not confined to, the suffering of neurotics whose perception of reality is distorted to the extent that they are capable of being upset by what other people would consider to be normal events. At a slightly deeper level, the awareness is dependent upon a perception of reality that is held in common by a particular group, and once again this includes but is not confined to the exclusive or xenophobic attitudes of certain extremists who do not accord equal humanity to everybody. But at the deepest level man is capable of an awareness of reality that transcends idiosyncracy and faction and approximates to the will of God. This approximation may be incomplete; the sense of wrongness that follows earthquakes or volcanic eruptions may be based on a less than complete understanding of God's will for the earth's crust. But it may also be that man is capable of being genuinely aware of when God's will has been abrogated, denied or consciously rejected, and of sharing in the pain that God feels at the outrage. And once a sharing in this particular pain has been consciously experienced, it can never again be denied.

The fourth and fifth aspects of man's uniqueness are to do with work. The first of these is the capacity for work itself. At the moment when man first discovered his capacity for choosing what he would do next, one of the things he must have realised was that he was capable of deciding not to do whatever was necessary to ensure his own survival. This has meant that ever since man has had to ensure his survival by means of exerting effort which he was capable of deciding not to exert, and this in turn has meant that ensuring his survival has become work. What man does to ensure his survival is thus different from the endless munching of grass by zebras or their instinctive running away from lions because zebras do not have the capacity to choose not to do these things. Once again, the book of Genesis encapsulates this anthropological moment; God tells Adam, after he and Eve have eaten the apple from the tree of the knowledge of good and evil, that from then on by the sweat of his brow he must toil to make bread. Zebras in this sense are still living in the Garden of Eden.

And finally there is man's unique capability for directing his work, for exercising his capacity for making choices when confronted by a job of work that needs to be done. Zebras, having no capacity for choice, are incapable of working out any way of feeding themselves beyond endless munching grass or of ensuring their survival beyond taking to their heels whenever a lion crosses the horizon. Man, on the other hand, is capable of thinking up a whole range of ways of feeding himself and of ensuring his security. His capacity for choice is the foundation of his intelligence, and because of it he is uniquely fitted to fulfil the divine charge of making order out of chaos and of cultivating the earth and making it fruitful. And once again, the fact that man is capable of working and of directing his work means that he has a need to work and to direct his work.

Any attempt to define work has first to take account of a distinction made in Pope John Paul II's 1981 encyclical *Laborem Exercens* between an objective view of work and a subjective view. The objective view looks at it from the standpoint of its end product, and thus sees it as worthwhile insofar as the results of it are worthwhile; if I make a cake, the work I put into it is validated by the end product being a cake that people can eat. Work in the objective sense may be defined as the effort a person puts into the conversion of those resources to which he as access, which in the case of the cake would be flour, sugar, eggs and a hot over, into something he needs, in this case a Victoria sponge. This is a definition that will be familiar to Marxists. The subjective view looks at the work from the point of view of the effect that doing it has upon the worker, and thus sees it as being worthwhile insofar as it enhances his personal self-fulfilment; if I enjoy making cakes and as a result of making them become a better cake-maker and a happier person, then the work I do is validated irrespective of whether or not anybody actually wants to eat my cakes. From this standpoint, the definition of work comes close to being whatever a person does when he is not doing something else; this is a definition that will be familiar to infant school teachers. Both the objective view and the subjective view present valid ways of looking at work and both offer valuable perspectives; it is the distinction that is important and in making it no judgement is implied as to relative significance.

Taking the objective view first, it is clear that there is work that needs to be done. In the first instance, work is necessary in order to ensure man's survival both as an individual and as a species, and it is the outcome of the work that matters rather than any fulfilling effect it may or may not have on the workers; in the immediate post-Eden period, hunting mammoths may or may not have been fun, but what would have mattered to people dependent on mammoth meat would have been a dead mammoth at the end of the day. There are three fundamental survival requirements, food, security, and scope for procreation.

The scope for procreation is important in that it affects the way that work is approached in human society rather than the nature of the work that is actually done. The instinctual patterns of behaviour that are programmed into all created species are designed to ensure the survival of the species rather than of its individual members; the way in which this works has been excitingly charted by Dr Richard Dawkins in his book *The Selfish Gene*. Procreation is clearly a prerequisite for the survival of the human species, but uniquely human beings have the capacity to choose not to do what is necessary in this respect. The importance of this for individual people is nothing to do with sexual habits or birth control, because there has never been a moment in history, at least during that part of it that social historians know about, when humanity has been at risk of extinction because of an insufficiency of impregnations. Its importance is to do with our attitude to groups. It seems clear that even during the pre-Eden period man was a gregarious animal and depended for survival upon group activities. Since Eden, man has remained gregarious, and his survival has depended upon his making decisions to accord a higher priority to the survival of his group than to the survival of himself as an individual. This explains the large number of instances in the history of mythology, from Phidipides to Colonel H Jones, where the heroic self-sacrifice of an individual for the benefit of his group has been commemorated.

One of the reasons why man is so gregarious is that the human young remain dependant for an exceptionally long time and responsibility for looking after them happens best as a shared activity; no doubt this is linked to the sheer quantity of information that the human young have to absorb before they are capable of becoming self-sufficient adults. And another reason, which has been mentioned before, is to do with man's need to practise and experience loving, which in its least sophisticated form is possible only in the context of group membership. Gregariousness implies that the benefits of work should accrue at least in part to the group as well as to individuals; food production should sufficient to ensure that the whole group survives and not just the active farmers, and security should require the survival of the group as a whole as well as of individual soldiers. Today it is generally accepted that a worker's wages should be spent for the benefit of his whole family, and also that a proportion of the aggregated wealth generated by work should be creamed off to enable certain services to be provided for the benefit of society as a whole; there are arguments about how great this proportion should be, but no arguments about the perpetuation of the principle.

The second basic requirement for survival is food, and the relationship between work and food is comparatively straightforward. In the early days the relationship was a direct one in theat work expended on hunting mammoths or tilling a field resulted in mammoth meat or a harvested crop. In the richer part of the world today, the relationship is indirect but equally straightforward in that the majority of workers are paid money for doing work that is unconnected with food production and then spend some of this money on buying food in supermarkets, but there are many variations on this relationship, for example when the money comes from social security payments rather than wages.

And the third basic survival requirement is security, which needs to be looked at from two points of view, external and internal. External security means protection against the elements, such as cold, rain, heat or earthquakes, and against predators such as lions or snakes; the work involved in this is largely a matter of building the right sort of houses and barricades. And external security also means protection against other groups of people since human beings are the only species apart from certain insects like ants that kill one another. The reason why man needs protection from his fellow creatures is largely to do with competition between different groups for access to the resources that are the raw material for work; for most of human history these resources have been in short supply and competition for access to them has often taken a violent form. The work involved takes the form either of diplomatic negotiation or of being prepared to fight, once again by certain members of the group on behalf of the group as a whole.

Internal security is to do with the group's cohesion. Many gregarious species such as zebras and baboons are instinctually programmed to live together cooperatively, and animal behaviourists such as Desmond Morris have recorded the huge variety of forms that this cooperation may take. Man retains a number of the cooperative instincts, but his gift of free will enables him to choose to behave in a way that is detrimental to the cohesion of the group; once again the motivation for such behaviour is often consequent upon his desire to have more than his allocated share of the group's resources. The ever-present possibility of such behaviour among its members means that the group has to protect itself against it, but first of all it needs to define the boundaries of what constitutes behaviour that is unacceptable. It also needs to define the obligations it considers necessary to impose upon its members, such as being prepared to undertake a share of the fighting in the event of attack, and foregoing a proportion of work or wealth for the general good. Once these definitions have been promulgated, there needs to be a system for identifying instances of behaviour that constitute a breach of what is considered acceptable, and for imposing sanctions upon those who are guilty of such a breach. The work involved in all this includes the whole panoply of government, of policing, and of the imposition of justice.

However work is not concerned solely with survival. Man's capacity for choosing how to direct his work and his capacity for applying his intelligence to what he does mean that in most circumstances he can do what is necessary to survive and still have time, energy and resources to spare. This is implied in the divine charge to cultivate the earth and make it fruitful, and it is the beginning of civilisation. Man can build himself houses that are comfortable to live in beyond the minimum requirements for keeping out the rain and the snakes, and he can develop methods of harvesting crops that increase the yield while minimising the work. This implies the development of tools and of new materials to make them with, and this in turn implies specialisation in work and the development of trade. Over the ages people have become increasingly aware of how they might channel their effort into meeting new needs that they had not realised existed before, and into improving the quality of their lives. Even in prehistoric times work had become complex.

And now something about work in its subjective sense. The fact that man has the capacity for work means that he needs to work, and the fact that he is also capable of directing his work means that he also has a need to apply his efforts constructively and creatively. One of the most endearing aspects of the creation story in Genesis chapter 1 is the way that at the end of each day's work God sits back with a sense of almost smug satisfaction and says, "That's good". Most people who have successfully completed a job of work that needed to be done have experienced this same sense of satisfaction, and it is an important ingredient in their self-fulfilment. If an individual is prevented by whatever circumstances from spending a proportion of this time in demanding and worthwhile activity, he will lose his sense of purpose and his individuality will begin to disintegrate. In the words of Pope John Paul II's Encyclical, work is that to which man "is predisposed by his very nature, by virtue of humanity itself . . . Only man is capable of work, and only man works, at the same time by work occupying his existence on earth . . . Man's life is built up every day from work, and from work it derives its special dignity." This is the fundamental truth at the heart of the subjective view of work, and it needs to be borne in mind whenever the objective view is considered. It has implications for the way that activity is organised in each individual workplace, and it has implications too for the way in which work is organised within society. It explains why the present high levels of unemployment, both in the western world and in the underdeveloped world, need to be taken so seriously; there is no shortage of worthwhile work that needs to be done, so there is an organisational challenge to society to find ways of enabling this work to be performed, and there is a psychological challenge to unemployed individuals to see empty hours as an opportunity for doing something creative and constructive as an alternative to doing very little and feeling unwanted and rejected.

So man needs to work, and there is plenty of work that needs to be done. Man would be denying his true nature if he were to look at the world without being filled with a strong urge to do something about it, and the divine charge to make order out of chaos and to cultivate the earth and make it fruitful is as good a way as any of describing this urge. And man would be denying his true nature if he were to think that he was capable of living his life through without devoting a significant proportion of his time and energy to demanding and purposeful activity. All this is by the way of saying that work, in both the objective and the subjective senses, is something that man needs to do and that it is God's will that he should do it. And in today's world a very high proportion of man's work happens within the context of paid employment. Work happens best if it is organised in some way, and paid employment is a good way of organising it; if paid employment didn't exist it would be necessary to invent it or something very like it, which probably explains why man managed to invent it in the first place. Paid employment provides man with a very important opportunity for worshipping God and for doing his will.

And finally, a thought about the limitations of work. Largely as the result of the accumulated outcome of centuries of effective work, man knows a great deal more about himself and about the world he lives in than at any previous time in his history. Developments in medical science have enabled him to understand a great deal about how his body works, developments in psychology have enabled him to understand a great deal about how his mind works and about how he relates to other people, and developments in sociology have enable him to understand a great deal about how he organises himself into groups. At the same time developments in technology have given him the ability to control a large number of aspects of the created world and to manipulate them to his advantage. All this creativity and inventiveness, which not only extend man's knowledge and power but also are proof of how creative and inventive he is, might have been expected to have increased his self-confidence and reinforced his belief in his own potential. But in spite of man as a species having demonstrated how good at work he is, there are still people starving or being tortured and every individual is still capable of feeling inadequate and insecure. Man is still frightened of pain, suffering and death. Loneliness, purposelessness, frustration and betrayal are still everyday realities. In part, this is a condemnation of man for having defined his work objectives wrongly and misapplied his work efforts, but in the main it is an indication of the limited parameters of work; the things that worry man most and contribute most to his unhappiness, and the things that he needs to do to overcome this worry and this unhappiness in preparation for becoming truly human, are not in the main matters that work can deal with however fulfilling it may be or how effectively it may be performed.

What this implies is that in order to be a successful human being it is necessary to do more than merely be successful at work, and that for a society to be successful it must take account of more than the successful ordering of work. However at this moment in time there is a risk of Christians becoming preoccupied with those aspects of the human condition that are not to do with work, while failing to appreciate that work too, including work undertaken in the course of paid employment, is just as much a proper area for their concern. Perceiving God's presence in the workplace is not easy, but he is undoubtedly there. A full awareness of his presence requires a framework within which the experiences of paid employment and the experiences of Christian belief can be integrated, and the bare bones of such a framework have been established in this chapter. Paid employment provides man with the scope for working and for applying his intelligence and creativity to his work, and for making his own particular contribution, however small, to sorting out the world's problems and developing its resources; all this is part of God's will both for makind in general and for each individual employee. But the framework needs to be developed further, and this cannot happen without a clear and honest appreciation of what paid employment actually is. The next four chapters attempt to help in this appreciation by exploring four important distinctions; their purpose is to clarify and there is no implication that the activities and processes that are compared are mutually incompatible or that the more impersonal half of each distinction is outside God's concern.

3

Distinction One: Religious Awareness and Rational Activity

One of God's special gifts to human beings is the gift of reason. This enables people to reflect upon their experiences and predicaments, and to construct frameworks which will make sense of the experiences and provide guidelines as to how the predicaments may best be coped with. It is a very valuable gift and provides the very basis for human civilisation and for the work upon which civilisation is grounded. However, in common with most gifts, reason has its darker side; it is capable of being used to distort as well as to clarify the meaning of what it is to be human, of what it is to be God's creation.

The distinction explored in this chapter is between religious awareness, which is to do with the fundamental business of being human, and rational activity, which is the use of only one aspect of human capability and which may be a comparatively superficial way of passing the time. Attempting a definition of the distinction is invidious, since the process of defining things is just about the most rational activity there is; defining things is a matter of using language very precisely, and the development of language and the development of the habit of precise thought are the end products of centuries of civilisation during which man has been refining his rational gifts. Religious awareness can only be hinted at in words; Wordsworth offers a glimpse of it in the *Immortality Ode:*

> Thanks to the human heart by which we live,
> Thanks to its tenderness, its joys and fears,
> To me the meanest flower that blows can give
> Thoughts that do often lie too deep for tears.

Shelley suggests how we are capable of it only indirectly:

> Life like a dome of many coloured glass
> Stains the white radiance of eternity.

Man, because he is both God's creation and gifted with reason, is capable of perceiving his experiences in two different

27

ways, and Arnold Toynbee in *An Historian's Approach to Religion* defines the distinction like this:

> In the Human Psyche there are two organs, a conscious volitional surface and a subconscious emotional abyss. Each of these two organs has its own way of looking at, and peering through, the dark glass that screens reality from man's inward eye, and in screening it, dimly reveals it; and therefore either imperfect mode of imperfect apprehension legitimately calls its findings "The Truth".

He goes on to examine the differences between the Truth of the Subconscious and the Truth of the Intellect, seeing the former as finding its natural expression in poetry and the latter in science, and he identifies one major difficulty:

> Poetry and Science have to use the same vocabulary, because man has only one vocabulary, and this therefore has to serve all man's purposes,

He then quotes T. S. Eliot's line from *Burnt Norton*:

> Words strain, crack and sometimes break under the burden.

Poetic truth is timeless in the sense that the nature of man's subconscious does not change over time, and any individual vision of it is capable of having an immediacy of meaning to later generations. The works of Sophocles and Shakespeare are as alive today as when they were written. Scientific truth, on the other hand, is cumulative in that one generation is capable of building upon the awareness of its forebears, and this means that the astronomy of Ptolomy and the anatomy of Leonardo da Vinci have to be rejected as inaccurate in the light of discoveries made by their successors. However the two types of truth inevitably blur at the edges, and in order to appreciate fully King Oedipus or King Lear we have to have at least a passing familiarity with the cultural environment in which they were created, and we can appreciate the imaginative vision of Ptolomy and Leonardo even though they came to only partially accurate conclusions.

The source of religion is the subconscious emotional abyss. Man's origin and purpose are capable of being understood only at a subconscious level, and though this understanding is capable of being articulated in conscious and rational terms, the conscious and the rational are incapable in themselves of providing answers to the deepest questions. The conscious and rational explanation of religious awareness, which is the province of theology, will distort that awareness if it ever becomes prey to its own self-contained logic and loses its connection with subconscious reality.

The distinction between religious awareness and rational activity is important in relation to paid employment because paid employment is almost totally a rational activity. Work has a primeval origin rooted in the processes of survival and in man's divine charge to cultivate the earth and make it fruitful, but now that work, in the rich quarter of the world at least, has developed into paid employment, survival and cultivation linger on only as atavistic memories amid a welter of of defined objectives, job descriptions and terms and conditions of service. The nature of these will be explored in the chapter that follows, but the point that needs to be made here is that defined objectives, job descriptions and terms and conditions of service have for the most part been carefully thought out, and if they haven't they should have been. When we do our work, we are pursuing a thought-out course and are using our own powers of reason. It is thus perfectly possible to spend a whole day sitting at a cash register or taking the minutes of a committee meeting without being aware of God's presence at all; indeed even the most Christian of managers would be justified in saying that if we were to spend the day ruminating upon God we would not be properly doing our job.

Making the distinction between religious awareness and rational activity is straightforward enough, but there are a number of aspects of the relationship between them that need to be developed further. The first is that the subconscious origin of our awareness of God does not mean that the conscious and the rational are outside his concern. The subconscious and the conscious are united in the sense that they coexist within a single person, and people in the entirety are God's creations. This means that we remain loved by God even when we are not thinking about him with our conscious minds. When we are engaged in rational activity such as clocking up merchandise on a cash register or taking the minutes of a meeting we are using some of our capabilities but not all of them, but those capabilities that we aren't using remain as much a part of us as if we were using them. Man's capability for rational activity is God-given, and God's concern is both that it be used and that it be used for his greater glory. Effective work is an aspect of worship in the sense that it represents God's gifts being put to good use irrespective of whether or not the gifts are attributed to the giver, and the sense of well-being that follows effective work is a form of thanksgiving whether or not it is expressed in Christian terms. In addition rational activity can be directly related to religious awareness in that it is capable of being applied in the task of clarifying and increasing our understanding of the nature of God, for example in the practice of theology or even in the writing or the reading of this book.

It also means that the subconscious and the conscious within a particular person need to be in harmony with each other. Even though most people most of the time may not be consciously aware of their subconscious selves, where the two are at variance with each other things start to go wrong. Reason is one of the gifts given to emotional man and he may use that gift as he chooses, but if he chooses to use it in a way that is out of kilter with his emotional heartland trouble will follow. Lady Macbeth's rational assessment of her predicament was that if Duncan were murdered she would become queen and the desirability of the end seemed to her to justify the means, but she failed to take into account the extent to which the murder would outrage her subconscious sense of morality and order, and she ended up with a mind deseased and blood indelibly on her hands. There are offences against the subconscious less dramatic than hers, for instance where promotion is given disproportionate priority to the detriment of friendships, or where so much energy is directed on work that all else withers.

The second important implication of the relationship between religious awareness and rational activity is that even though the source of religious awareness is the subconscious emotional abyss, not everything within the abyss is to do with religion. It is possible to be influenced by the subconscious and become motivated by a whole variety of impulses some of which may be very destructive; indeed one of the stumbling in the promulgation of religion is the appalling catalogue of destruction that has been perpetrated in God's name. The proponents of the Spanish inquisition saw it as God's will that they should burn infidels and the Yorkshire Ripper saw it as God's will that he should murder prostitutes. It is only during the last hundred years that man has embarked upon the methodical charting of the subconscious, and even though further progress will probably be made it seems unlikely that the subconscious will ever be fully understood; indeed the very progress of its charting is itself a rational activity and there is always the risk that the rational desire to compress our limited awareness into logical patterns will distort our understanding of its true nature. Nevertheless the work of Freud and his successors has shown that man's subconscious is the source of destructive urges which may or may not be expressed in destructive action, and which if suppressed may be manifested in action that is both destructive and bizarre. And it has also shown how the destructiveness may be compounded by unsatisfactory experiences particularly of being inadequately loved during early childhood. And yet the subconscious remains the source of our awareness of God. It is possible for us to disarm destructive emotions by understanding and accepting them, and it is also possible for us to see straight to the still centre of the abyss where God's presence is most clearly perceived and so discount these destructive emotions by appreciating their comparative unimportance. And the emotions with which the abyss is populated are not all destructive; Freud was fully aware of the power of love, and though he tended to link it with the needs for sexual expression, status and self-definition, he and his successors were able to see too that it is capable of taking a self-sacrificial form enabling selfhood to be most fully expressed by being denied.

The third point about religious awareness and rational activity is that, if every person has a subconscious, it must follow that every person has a capacity for religious awareness, and this has a profound relevance for Christian mission. There are, of course, large numbers of people, Christians and non-Christians alike, who need to pretend that the abyss does not exist, probably because some unnamed horror in their history which makes the admission of its existence intolerable. The probable result is that they will attempt to live out their lives on the superficial assumption that existence is capable of being reduced to purely rational terms, and they will concoct a rational explanation for those aspects of their attitudes and behaviour that are motivated from within the abyss which will preclude them from ever understanding the full nature of that motivation. There is a further group of people who allow themselves to see some distance into the abyss without seeing as far as the still centre; their conclusion will probably be that the subconscious is dangerous and to be understood only insofar as understanding it is a prerequisite for avoiding the dangers. This attitude, which can sadly be the end-product of the experience of psychoanalysis, will often lead to an attempt to establish purely rational goals which, however helpful and viable they may be within their appropriate circumscribed fields, leave whole areas of existence untouched. And there are also people who are capable of seeing to the still centre but who do not articulate that experience in Christian terminology or relate it to Christian doctrine or ritual. There are some who have found the terminology of Eastern religions helpful and who have sustained their experience by means of Eastern meditation techniques, but one of the consequences of this sort of framework is that it is very difficult to find within it a place for the rational experiences of paid employment, harder even than it is within Christianity. And there are others who develop their own frameworks, for example those who combine contemplation with walking the dog without appreciating what contemplation is or where it leads; the difficulty for them is likely to be that their religious awareness will be very vulnerable to changes in personal routine such as illness, retirement, or even the death of the dog.

Nevertheless, religious awareness is a great bond between people whatever the framework within which they choose to express it. The value of Christianity is that it provides a well charted framework which is capable of sustaining religious awareness throughout the whole spectrum of personal predicaments; this book suggests not only how that framework can be extended to include the experience of paid employment but also how that extension can be beneficial to the framework as a whole. The business of making frameworks is itself a rational activity, and if a framework can embrace an activity as rational as paid employment it will serve also to enhance those elements that are rooted in religious awareness.

And the fourth and most important implication is that rational activity, whether it be in the course of paid employment or in theology or in the writing or reading of books, needs to be constantly referred back to religious awareness in order to ensure that it remains consistent with our deepest experiences, those that are capable of translation into words only in parables, metaphors and symbols; rational activity needs to be constantly under-girded by prayer.

4

Distinction Two: People and Institutions

Most work happens in the context of paid employment and most paid employment happens in the context of institutions. The distinction which this chapter seeks to establish is between people on the one hand, who are created by God for purposes which he alone knows, and institutions on the other, which are created for human beings for purposes which human beings have defined.

Work is normally undertaken in groups, partly because man is a gregarious animal anyway, and partly because, as anyone who has attempted to move a piano single-handed will appreciate, group activity is capable of being more efficient and effective than individual activity. Perhaps there was once a time when groups of people did all their work together, going off to hunt mammoths when mammoth meat was needed, tilling the fields at tilling time and harvesting the crops at harvest time, and repelling invaders whenever invasion threatened. However as society became more sophisticated, so work tended to become more specialised; a blacksmith would make metal tools for the whole community which he would exchange for food so that he would not have to go off farming with everybody else. As specialised work became more sophisticated, so it required the cooperation of a group of people who would come together to get the work done without necessarily coming together for any other purpose; metal tools are now made by a large number of people working together in a factory who do not necessarily meet each other outside working hours. An institution is a group of people coming together for the limited purpose of getting something particular done.

Before embarking upon a discussion of the nature of institutions, it would be helpful to distinguish between two different types, representative and commercial. Institutions of the first type are set up because a number of people identify a need for their interests to be protected or furthered in some way.

If people are to live successfully together, there needs to be some accepted system for making decisions that affect the community as a whole; representative institutions in their most obvious form are those that exist by virtue of the consent of the community to take action on the community's behalf, like the House of Commons and local authorities. Then there are institutions like the civil service and local authority bureancracies whose function is to ensure that these decisions are implemented. One of the tasks of decision-making institutions is to decide what services should be provided for the benefit of the community as a whole, and to finance these by means of creaming off a proportion of the community's wealth, for example through taxes or rates. In Chapter 2 reference was made to a community's need for external security, and the armed forces are an example of a representative institution. Examples of representative institutions that are concerned with internal security are the policy forces, the criminal courts, and the prison system. A sophisticated society also tends to want to regulate certain of its affairs, and to set up institutions like the civil courts, the Equal Opportunities Commission, and the Milk Marketing Board. And a sophisticated society also tends to want to ensure that adequate provision is made to keep its members healthy, wealthy and wise, so it sets up institutions like the National Health Service, the social security system and local education authorities, and these in turn set up institutions like hospitals, DHSS local offices and schools.

There are some representative institutions which do not exist by virtue of a decision made on behalf of the community as a whole, but which are set up to protect and further the interests of particular subgroups within the community. Trade unions like the TGWU, professional bodies like the Royal College of Physicians, pressure groups like the National Campaign for Nursery Education, interest groups like the Trainspotter's Association and community groups like the Belgravia Residents' Association; all of these are examples of representative institutions.

Mention was made earlier of blacksmiths making metal tools, and this can still be done by individuals working alone, but making things like cars or washing machines are such complex operations that it is impossible to imagine them being made except by institutions. These institutions are commercial, and even a blacksmith nowadays would have difficulty in selling his tools except through a commercial institution like a shop. Whereas representative institutions are financed for the most part by money that the community has decided should be creamed off from its individual members' wealth, commercial institutions are financed for the most part as a result of individuals deciding to cream off a proportion of their own wealth to pay for the goods or services that the institution has on offer. Representative institutions come to an end when those they represent decide that the institution is no longer required; commercial institutions come to an end when individuals are no longer willing to part with enough of their own wealth to keep the institution in business. This means that the existence of the former is authenticated only so long as they are seen to be operating in the community's or the group's best interest, and that the existence of the latter is authenticated only so long as they remain commercially viable. These are important points that need to be born in mind, even though things aren't always as clear cut as this in practice; there are plenty of examples of representative institutions that manage to perpetuate their existence by exploiting the political system or because of the political system's particular quirks, and there are some commercial institutions that continue in business even when they make a loss because of political decisions to subsidise them, and others which are closed down by political decisions for example if they are thought to be socially harmful.

This brief examination of different types of institution does not aim to be comprehensive, it merely aims to give some indication as to what institutions are as a preliminary to an analysis of their nature and their essential characteristics. The first characteristic of institutions is that they translate perceived needs into work. Institutions are set up for the purpose of meeting a perceived need. They then set themselves objectives, and these objectives are met by means of the successful performance of defined tasks, and the performance of these tasks is somebody's work. A washing machine factory will be set up to meet the perceived need of people to save their time and energy which would otherwise be spent washing clothes by hand, and its purpose will be to build washing machines at a price that people are prepared to pay. Its objectives will include building a hundred Type X machines by next Tuesday, and Joe Smith's tasks will include putting the knobs onto each one. A school will be set up to meet the perceived need for the children in the area to be educated, and its purpose will be to educate the children. Its objectives will include enabling a particular group of thirty children to learn about chemistry, and Mr Smith's tasks will include teaching chemistry to Form 3B second period on Wednesday afternoon. The Central Criminal Court was set up to meet the need for guilt to be established in instances where unacceptable behaviour had been alleged, and its purpose is to ensure that defendants receive a fair trial. One of its objectives might be to establish whether or not Jim Brown had committed the robbery with which he had been charged, and the tasks of his Honour Judge Smith would include presiding over R. v Brown on Thursday.

The second characteristic of institutions is that they confer a role upon the people who are involved in their functions. Whatever the various Smiths may have had for breakfast or done the evening before, the moment they step into their institution at nine o'clock in the morning they become a knob fitter, a chemistry teacher, or a High Court Judge. And the children in 3B become pupils, and Jim Brown becomes a defendant. And when they leave the institution at the end of the day, they step out of their role, though if Jim Brown receives a custodial sentence he will enter another institution and assume a different role, that of a prisoner. And as well as confering a role, institutions also confer status. Within a school, the pupils will at least to some extent defer to the teacher by virtue of the teacher's status, and the teachers will at least to some extent defer to the head, while in the court room everybody will rise as the judge enters in symbolic deference to his status and will carry out his orders in actual deference. This status is conferred by the institution and is for the duration of assumption of the institutional role, though in practice people are quite likely to defer to the judge as he walks his dog in the park. And as well as confering role and status, institutions also confer power. Teachers are in a position to make pupils do things, and in order to make this power stick they have at their disposal incentives like gold stars or good references, and sanctions like detentions or bad references. Institutional power isn't the only sort of power; power also derives from personality, from ability, and from wealth, but institutional power is important and needs to be borne in mind in any consideration of paid employment.

The third characteristic of institutions is that they imply their own standards of attitude and conduct. In the first instance, they require that assigned tasks will be performed competently, since if they aren't the institution's objectives will not be achieved, its purposes will not be fulfilled, and the needs will not be met. If Joe Smith puts the knobs on wrong the washing machines won't work, no one will buy them, the factory will go bankrupt, and people will have to continue doing their washing by hand. If Mr Smith makes a mess of his 3B chemistry lesson the children won't learn what they are meant to, the school will have failed and the children will end up not properly educated. If His Honour Judge Smith makes mistakes while presiding over the trial Jim Brown will not get a fair hearing and justice will not have been seen to have been done.

But institutions are as much concerned with the future as with the present. Attitudes and conduct need not just to ensure the competent performance of current tasks, but also to take account of the longer term; the standards that institutions require of their employees need to ensure that the institution continues in business tomorrow. This places an imperative upon a proper respect for people and resources, and means that account has to be taken of the points made earlier, that the continued existence of representative institutions is dependant upon their retaining their constituencies' confidence by demonstrating that the constituencies' interests continue to be served, and that the continued existence of commercial institutions is dependant upon their remaining commercially viable.

This combination of present and future institutional requirements add up to what are sometimes referred to as institutional ethics. What matters are competence and other people's trust, both in the short and in the longer term. A mammoth hunter needs to understand mammoths sufficiently well to know the point at which a mammoth is particularly susceptible to a spear-thrust, and he needs to understand spears sufficiently well to know that a fire-hardened one is more effective than one that has been merely flint-sharpened; otherwise he will not be able to kill mammoths. But at the same time he needs to understand mammoths sufficiently well to know that if he overhunts them there will be no more mammoths to hunt tomorrow. A barley farmer needs to understand barley seeds sufficiently well to know that they are most likely to germinate if planted in April after rain, while at the same time appreciating that if the field is overcropped there is a risk that it might not support a harvest next year. In a factory, a lathe operator needs to understand both his lathe and his metal so that he can get the best out of them, and his foreman needs to understand how to get the best out of the lathe operators, but both need to appreciate that if they push matters too far there is a risk of the lathe breaking down or the workforce walking out so that tomorrow's productivity will be nil. And there is no point in a hunter knowing all about how to fire-harden spears if he doesnt have the skill to stick one in where it matters, or in a schoolteacher understanding all about his subject if he has no classroom skills. A general practitioner needs not only to exercise his medical knowledge and his diagnostic skills, but also to win his patient's confidence so that the patinet will come back the next time he feels ill; if everybody lost confidence in their doctors there would be a general regression to quack remedies and the family practitioner service as an institution would wither away. In commerce, competent performance will lead to increased trading, but when people are doing business together, whether it be over the shop counter, across the negotiating table, or on the floor of the stock exchange, they need to be able to proceed on the assumption that certain basic rules of conduct will be observed; a breach of trust my yield a quick profit, but it will jeopardise future transactions.

Institutions enforce these ethical standards in a variety of ways. One way is through selection; all employers look for a potential for understanding and skill during the process of recruitment. Another is through training; most put some effort into giving employees the opportunity for developing their potential. A third is through promotion, which is normally offered on the basis of potential having been realised, partly because this is a sensible criterion, and partly as an encouragement to high standards in others. And a fourth is that all exercise some form of discipline in matters of incompetence or misconduct. Disciplinary procedures are instituted not only because certain behaviour or attitudes are in themselves wrong as because, if left uncensored, they would jeopardise the institution's future. The General Medical Council strikes delinquent doctors off the register not only because of any inherent wickednesses in their deliquencies, but also because their delinquencies might bring the medical profession into disrepute and damage public confidence.

Some people have a tendency to disparage institutional ethics as being somehow less lofty than ethics derived from some other source. The standards required by institutions are in fact admirable and very demanding, but it is true that their justification is circular; mammoth hunters need to understand both how to kill mammoths and when not to because such understanding is a necessary part of mammoth hunting, and stock brokers need both to anticipate skilfully the movements of commodity prices and eschew insider dealing dealing because both are intrinsic to the broking of stocks. If farmers overcropped their fields there would be no more farming, and if litigants felt that they couldn't trust their lawyers they wouldn't bother to hire them. No one would want to hunt mammoths with someone who was likely to run away at the crucial charge, and no one would want to do business with a wholesaler who was known to supply shoddy goods. The details of the ethical standards that are required by different institutions will vary according to the nature of the institution's purpose and the tasks that it requires to be performed, but the principles that underpin the ethics seem universal; what matters is that both today's and tomorrow's objectives should be achieved. The standards required are very high and of course they are not always met, but it is important to appreciate that they exist and that they exist by virtue of the existence of the institution.

And the fourth characteristic of institutions is that they are not people; in particular, they are incapable of human feelings and attitudes. There is always a tendency to anthropomorphise institutions, and to attribute to them human characteristics; it is misleading and unhelpful to say, for example, that the social security system doesn't care, or that a particular school or hospital is loving, or that a particular police force hates ethnic

41

minorities. The institutions have specific purposes and objectives such as to distribute payments according to defined criteria, or to teach chemistry or mend hernias, or to reduce crime and apprehend suspected criminals, and these tasks are capable of being performed either well or badly. There are, inevitably, instances of DHSS desk clerks who perform their tasks grudgingly or rudely, teachers who are disparaging and doctors who are insensitive, and policemen who overstep the mark when dealing with coloured youngsters, but in each case it is the employees who are at fault in behaving in breach of the institution's ethical standards. Such instances need to be followed up with disciplinary action, and if they aren't the institution is failing in the fulfilment of its purpose. There is, of course, a great deal of scope for individuals both within and outside an institution to influence the way that an institution reacts to such instances, and equally there are individuals who go beyond the requirements of institutional ethics to be especially considerate, but these are the contributions of individual people and not characteristics of the institution.

Another instance where it is wrong to think in terms of an institution expressing human emotions is in an institution's relationship with its staff. An institution is incapable of caring for its staff since its sole concern is that they perform their tasks competently and in accordance with the appropriate ethical requirements. This concern for competent performance is not able to take account of the fact that one person may have a headache or that another may have to go to the dentist or that another may have a personal phobia about using the telephone. Individual managers may be more or less sympathetic to such problems and may be willing to be more or less flexible in making arrangements for them to be taken into account, but the institution's sole concern is that the work gets done. Insofar as an institution is generous to its staff, this is only in the context of a contractual relationship (more about contracts later), and this generosity is only for the duration of a person's usefulness as an employee; if he stops being useful he has to be dismissed. Insofar as the dismissal is conducted humanely or with sweeteners, this also is in the context of contractual procedures perhaps negotiated by trade unions representing the interests of other staff who are may be anxious about the possibility of their own dismissals. In saying all this there is no intention to imply that institutions are of necessity brutal (brutal is another anthropomorphic word); the intention is merely to underline the important distinction between institutions and people.

An even more important way in which institutions are different from people is that they have different origins. Institutions have a purpose that has been defined by human beings, and therefore that purpose is capable of being understood by human beings. The initial purpose of some of the more ancient institutions like the Worshipful Company of Fishmongers may have become obscured by the mists of time, and some institutions may have changed their purposes or developed new ones, but both the initial and current purposes of institutions are capable of human comprehension, even if the unravelling of them may be somewhat complex. Human beings, on the other hand, are created by God, and the purpose of human beings is beyond the comprehension or definition of even the most ambitious psychologist or sociologist. This distinction has profound implications particularly for the assessment of success or failure. Since man has defined and is capable of understanding the purposes of institutions, he is capable of assessing the extent to which these purposes are or are not being fulfilled. When failure occurs it is capable of being remedied by means of institutional reform which man is capable of implementing. Man, on the other hand, is incapable of comprehending the purpose that had been defined for him; failure to fulfil it is inevitable at least some of the time, and the remedy that is perpetually necessary is by the mysterious processes of repentance and redemption. More later also on this.

It is worth at this stage saying something about a number of borderline institutions. Is a family an institution? Is a congregation? Is the Church? The answer in all of these cases is both yes and no. The two questions it is helpful to ask are whether a person is embodying a role or being himself, and whether or not it is important that his tasks be performed competently. Within a family a person is called upon to embody a role for some of the time, most obviously that of father or mother, and their are certain tasks that are expected of fathers and mothers in the same way that there are certain tasks expected of knobfitters, teachers and Crown Court judges; if

43

these tasks are not performed, the family suffers. However families exist primarily in order to enable their members to be more fully themselves as individuals, and the relationships and responsibilites provide the context within which this fulfilment is able to happen. There are clearly a number of family tasks where competence matters, like putting nappies properly onto babies, mending the washing machine so that it actually works and buying the right things at the supermarket, but the point about a family meal, say, is not so much that it should necessarily be competently cooked but that it should happen as a family occasion.

The same distinctions apply within a congregation; clergy, church wardens and PCC members all have certain roles to embody, though apart from a small number of formal occasions this matters a great deal less than their common membership as individuals of a worshipping community. And what matters about the Eucharist is that it happens; it is a pity when the vicar mumbles his words or when the choir sings flat, but this is as unimportant as overdone sprouts at a family Sunday lunch. On the other hand there is no reason for incompetence when it comes to getting the chancel roof mended or appointing a new teacher to the voluntary aided primary school. The Church as a whole needs to operate as a competent institution most obviously when it is concerned with the training and employment of its staff and when looking after its buildings and its finances; the fact that all of these are secondary to its primary purpose as the body of Christ is no excuse for incompetence.

However this book is primarily about paid employment, and this chapter ends with some statements about the nature of institutions as employers. Employees enter voluntarily into a contract of employment with their employing institution under which the institution agrees to do a certain number of things for the employee, most obviously to pay him money, and the employees agree to do a certain number of things for the institution, most obviously to work. One thing that the employee agrees to do is to make available to the institution a specified proportion of his time. Another is that he agrees to perform the tasks that the institution requires in accordance with agreed ethical standards, and this will make demands upon his energy, skills, and judgement. This degree of commitment necessitates at least to some extent adopting the institution's values, believing the institution's objectives to be important; a washing machine salesman will have difficulty doing his job effectively if he has not convinced himself that people are better off with a washing machine than without one. And the employee also agrees to assume the role that the institution requires of him; a Crown Court judge must interpret the law and a civil servant must implement the policies of the Government of the day, irrespective of what they as individuals might otherwise have chosen to do in the circumstances.

The obligations that a person assumes when he enters into a contract of employment are examined in greater detail in the chapter that follows; the point that is made here is that these obligations are capable of causing difficulties for committed Christians and it would be a dangerous mistake to suppose that they don't. The time commitment means that during the hours that a person is contracted to be about his employer's business he ceases to be free to respond spontaneously to situations where he might suppose that God had called him to do something else. A commitment to the values of an institution is not necessarily in itself objectionable from a Christian standpoint, but it is certainly different from a commitment to the values that are traditionally associated with Christian belief; the classic dilemma for Christian managers is when they are called upon to dismiss a member of staff whose weaknesses they understand and are sympathetic to but which are incompatible with the achievement of the institution's objectives. And the commitment to an institutional role, though once again not in itself objectionable, is different from the traditionally defined obligations of Christian witness, letting our light so shine before men that they may see our good works and glorify our Father which is in heaven. What Christians need to do is to extend the framework of their faith so that institutions are seen as just as much a part of God's world as everything else and are not excluded from it on the grounds that they are humanly created, and that what people do in the course of their paid employment is seen as just as much a part of doing God's will as everything else and is not excluded from it on the grounds that it is constrained by contractual requirements.

5

Distinction Three: Loving and the Successful Performance of Institutional Tasks

This chapter is concerned with establishing a distinction between loving and the successful performance of institutionally defined tasks. The obligations that bind a person when he chooses to enter into a contract of employment are compared with the obligations that become apparent to a person who appreciates the extent to which he is loved by God, and what motivates a person in the effective performance of his institutional tasks is compared with what motivates a person in expressing his response to God's love.

The previous chapter ended with a brief reference to contracts of employment in order to make the point that such contracts impose constraints upon the people who enter into them and that these may conflict with other things these people might wish to do, but there is more to contracts of employment than this. A contract of employment is a two-way agreement between an institution and an employee which makes binding obligations on both parties. The most obvious undertaking made by the institution is that it agrees to pay the employee a defined amount of money which the employee is then able to spend as he chooses, for example on feeding and housing himself and his family and on providing himself and his family with the scope for self-fulfilment outside working hours. And since contracts of employment are recognised in law, the institution is also bound by a number of statutory provisions including Sections 54 to 80 of the Employment Protection (Consolidation) Act 1978 which obliges employers not to dismiss their staff unfairly. These particular provisions give the employee a double security; not only does he get the security that comes with his pay cheque, but he also gets the security of knowing that unless circumstances arise which would permit his fair dismissal the pay cheques will keep coming in. And contracts of employment also often include other obligations on employing institutions which benefit the employee such as entitlements to annual leave and sick pay, and perhaps also to a number of those benefits in kind which are sometimes referred to as perks. There may also be other benefits included in the contract which have been negotiated by trade unions acting on the employee's behalf.

However, this chapter is primarily concerned with the obligations that contracts of employment impose upon employees, and the first of these is that employees undertake to perform those tasks that the institution requires of them, whether it be to put knobs on washing machines, to teach chemistry to Form 3B, or to preside over a trial at the Old Bailey. Some tasks are defined very specifically; for example there are not many different ways of putting a knob on a washing machine. But others are defined very open endedly; a chemistry teacher, for instance, has a great deal of latitude within his classroom because his task is to educate the children in chemistry and this is a much broader business than the mere recitation of a number of specified chemical facts. He needs to understand the way that children learn, and he is perfectly entitled to illustrate his chemistry with metaphors from grand opera if he is an opera afficianado and thinks it would help. If he chooses to do this he will be drawing on his personal experiences within the opera house, which in a sense is going beyond a strict interpretation of his institutional task, but the point is that he is entitled to do it only insofar as it is compatible with his institutional objective; the moment he loses sight of the children's educational needs and starts using them as fodder for an operatic ego trip he is failing in his institutional task and is in breach of his contract of employment.

And there are some institutional tasks that are more loosely defined even than school teaching. A washing machine company, for example, may decide to send somebody to Nigeria with the objective of creating a climate of opinion within Nigeria that will pave the way for Nigerians coming to the conclusion that washing machines are what they have always wanted. He may decide that the best way of setting about his task and achieving his objective is to go and live a remote Nigerian village for six months so that he can develop an understanding of its cultural patterns, and that during this time he will not mention washing machines at all. This would be an interesting experience for him, and would require that he draw upon whole areas of his experience that had nothing to do with his employing institution, and would be fine as long as he retained his commitment to selling washing machines in the longer term. It would also be fine if the conclusion he came to at the end of the six months was that selling washing machines to Nigerian villagers would be a fruitless exercise, though if a year later a rival company were to move in and sweep the board, this would be evidence of his gross misjudgement and of breach of contract on grounds of incompetence. If, however, his conclusion was that washing machines might well sell but that a concerted sales campaign would destroy the village's traditions and culture, it would be wrong for him to recommend that no campaign be mounted. If he felt that his commitment to the village took priority over his commitment to his institutional task, he would need to ask to be transferred or to resign.

It is also worth making the point that an institution, within certain constraints, has the right to alter the tasks that its employees are required to perform if circumstances arise which mean that the institution needs to redefine its objectives. If a new form of electric bus were to be developed that was more cost-effective and efficient than buses powered by diesel fuel, a bus company might need to require its drivers to move over to driving the new type of bus as part of a policy for keeping abreast of the times and remaining commercially viable. And if the electric buses were so efficient that they required much less maintenance, the company might need to get rid of a number of its maintenance engineers; Section 57 of the Employment Protection (Consolidation) Act recognises redundancy as grounds for fair dismissal. Of course it is always traumatic for staff to lose their jobs in such circumstances, and it is legitimate for trade unions on behalf of their members to campaign against redundancies and to negotiate with employing institutions procedures designed to render dismissals less traumatic; these procedures would then become part of the contract of employment.

Contracts of employment also give institutions the right to assume that the tasks that have been defined will be performed competently. Since an institution has a vested interest in competent performance, it will recruit only those people who are likely to perform competently, and this means that in staff selection special attention will be paid to people's abilities, skills and experience; applicants who do not impress in these respects will not be taken on. The institution will also wish to reward those employees whose competence is proved in actual performance, for example by means of bonus payments or promotion. And it also means that an employee who does not perform his appointed tasks competently is deemed to be in breach of his contract of employment and is liable to be disciplined or sacked; the Employment Protection (Consolidation) Act also allows incompetence as grounds for fair dismissal. And the institution's need to ensure competent performance also extends to factors that are in no sense the fault of a particular employee such as sickness or old age; the institution needs to get its work done and if an employee is too ill or infirm to manage the necessary tasks is unlikely to wish to keep him on. Within most institutions sickness and old age are the subject of agreed procedures which ensure that the impact of a person losing, say, his health and his job simultaneously are made somewhat less than catastrophic, but this does not affect the basic principle that an institution is under no obligation to employ staff who for whatever reason are unable to hold down their job.

Some people accuse institutions of being unfeeling or un-Christian in the rigidity of their requirement for competent performance. It is inevitable that there should be some managers who impose disciplinary sanctions or initiate dismissal proceedings inflexibly or viciously, but such managers are probably themselves in breach of contract in that their inflexibility or viciousness is unlikely to be compatible with the effective exercise of their responsibilities or with the institution's best interests. It is nevertheless unhelpful to make such accusations since institutions cannot feel and are incapable of being Christian. And an important point is that keeping an incompetent employee on is unlikely to help the employee in the longer term since people need to be made aware of their limitations and doing a job badly is not fun.

And a third element of contractual obligation is that an employee undertakes to abide by his employing institution's ethical standards. At its most basic level, this means that an employee's behaviour in the workplace must not be such as would jeopardise the successful performance of the institution's tasks. The Employment Protection (Consolidation) Act also recognises misconduct as grounds for fair dismissal, and misconduct covers vandalism, pilfering, unrecorded absenteeism and fiddling timesheets and expense accounts as well as the sort of rudeness or aggression that makes it harder for other people to do their jobs. At a slightly more lofty level, it means that an employee's conduct must not be such as might bring the institution into disrepute; this includes behaviour that for other people in other circumstances would be perfectly acceptable, such as solicitors advertising for business, civil servants allowing themselves to be interviewed by newspapers, or doctors dating patients. But on a higher level still, a contract of employment goes further than merely obliging an employee not to do the wrong thing; there is also a positive expectation that he will make a commitment to the institution and its values and will assume the required institutional role. An institution has the right to expect that a washing machine salesman, for example, will behave in accordance with the assumption that people are better off with washing machines than without them, and a teacher is expected to behave on the assumption that it is a good thing for children to come to school; if employees can't make commitments of this sort, they be in breach of their contract of employment even though this might be difficult to prove before an industrial tribunal, and they should consider very seriously whether they ought to resign. A policeman, to take another example, cannot walk down a street and turn a blind eye to a crime that is being committed, partly because one of his tasks is to apprehend suspected offenders, but also because the role of a policeman includes being a visible deterrent to the commission of crime. If a policeman were seen not to be doing something about a crime committed in front of his nose, public confidence in policing would diminish and the visible deterrent aspect of the policeman's role would be eroded. For this reason policemen are expected to intervene to deter crime and apprehend offenders even when they are off duty.

What is remarkable about paid employment is the extent to which most people most of the time do their jobs conscientiously and well, thus meeting all the obligations placed on them by their contracts of employment. What is it that motivates them in this? In prehistoric times, the motivation for effective work must have been obvious; effective work meant prosperity and security, while ineffective work or idleness meant penury and probably death. The relationship between work and survival has since become less direct, in the developed world at least, as a consequence of humanitarian intervention by the state. Nevertheless, the way in which most people would probably explain their commitment to their paid employment would be to say that they needed the money in order to be able to buy the food and pay the rent or the mortgage and the fuel bills necessary to ensure their own and their families' survival. If it were then pointed out to them that the state would never let them starve or go homeless, they would probably say that the benefits afforded by a contract of employment outweighed the costs; money and security are very desirable even if acquiring them means getting up earlier in the morning than a person might otherwise wish, followed by a bit of hard graft. And they would then probably list the useful and pleasurable things that money is able to buy.

Without denying that money is a significant motivation for work, it is probable that for most people it is not the primary motivation. Man needs to work, and he needs to apply to his work his intelligence and his creativity. It is intrinsic to the nature of man that he should spend some of his time in the constructive performance of worthwhile tasks, and institutional employment furnishes him with the scope for doing exactly this. What motivates a person to fulfil his contract of employment is thus essentially the same as what motivates him to do God's will, and there is a sense in which anything short of a wholehearted commitment, as well as being in breach of contract, is also sinful in that it renders him somewhat less than his true self. The fact that there are very few people who would express this in this way does not in itself mean that it is necessarily untrue. It is nonetheless interesting that the history of the Labour Movement has been dominated by demands for the right to work rather than for the right to a guaranteed income; no trade union or Labour Party manifesto has seen having an income without work as being preferable to doing a job even at the same wage, and the experience of unemployment suggests that the deprivation of something constructive to do is more damaging than any diminution of income. It is also interesting that in Communist countries the policy for dealing with unemployment is to create artificial jobs for people to do rather than to pay them a dole; this at least gives people the opportunity for activity, but the fact that the artificiality of some of the jobs seems to give rise to its own brand of resentment suggests that what matters is not so much the need for activity but the need for activity that is appreciated as worthwhile.

A third aspect of what motivates people in their paid employment is that it provides them with a framework for their lives and gives them the security of being able to order their existence. The gift to man of the capacity to make choices has always been something of a two-edged blessing, and having to make decisions is a burden and a responsibility as well as a privilege and an opportunity. Once a person has entered into a contract of employment a large number of decisions are effectively made for him; the time he has to get up in the morning is determined by the time he is required to present himself for work, the way he dresses is determined by the institution's culture, what he does during working hours is determined by the nature of his institutional tasks, and what he does outside working hours is determined to a considerable extent by the income, the status and the role that the institution confers upon him. One of the reasons why unemployment is so often debilitating is because it destroys the day-shaping framework that a contract of employment provides, and throws the responsibility for minute-by-minute decisions back onto the person concerned; this responsibility may be overwhelming for somebody whose self-confidence is already likely to be low. The instinct a person has to allow his existence to be externally shaped and to surrender his decision-making capacity to an external power is deep-seated.

There are two further aspects of this motivation that are worth mentioning, and both relate to doing work well rather than merely to doing it. The first of these, which amplifies and extends the money motivation, is to do with institutional ambition and with institutional status and power. One of the responsibilities of institutions is to appoint to particular posts people who have the aptitudes, skills and experience necessary for the performance of the appropriate tasks, and one method of recruitment is by promotion. People who want to be promoted will be anxious to demonstrate that they have the aptitudes, skills and experience appropriate for a post at a greater level of responsibility, and will be motivated to raise the level of their performance above the merely competent. Such aspirations may be prompted by people recognising within themselves aptitudes that are under-used, and this may cause them to seek to complement these aptitudes by acquiring additional skills and experience so that they will be equipped to perform more responsible and complex tasks at a higher level and thus be provided with the scope for putting themselves more comprehensively into practice. Or they may be prompted solely by the fact that promotion normally carries with it more money, higher status and increased power, and these may be thought to be worth having either for their own sakes or as a means towards something else.

And the final aspect of this motivation is an amplification and extension of man's need to direct his work. An institution requires of a person at least a minimum degree of competence, but there are some tasks that are capable of being performed to a degree of competence that is very much higher. What motivates a person to raise the level of his performance to this higher level goes beyond institutional requirement or institutional ambition; it is the expression of a need in man to pursue excellence for its own sake. This is in part a manifestation of man's need to apply his intelligence and his creativity to his work, but in a sense it goes beyond even this. In the same way that efective work is a means of worshipping God, so also is the pursuit of excellence.

The pursuit of excellence within paid employment is a process which is dictated by the nature of the tasks that have to be performed, and because of this the vision of what is excellent has to be communally held by all who are called upon to perform those particular tasks. In most of the so called "professions", there is an accepted understanding of what constitutes "good practice"; there is a communally held vision of how nursing procedures ought to be carried out, of how solicitors should conduct themselves, and of what is expected of a soldier. Any attempt by any individual nurse, solicitor or soldier to achieve individual excellence has to be constrained by what is required of her or him in their calling. In all branches of paid employment the ideals of performance are similarly defined, and though the definition may be couched in loftier terms in the case of civil servants or members of the stock exchange than in the case of washing machine knobfitters, it is no doubt possible to envisage an excellent way of fitting knobs. However even though these visions of what is excellent are communally defined and are dictated by the nature of the tasks involved, it is up to each individual worker to chart and to follow his own individual road towards approximating to them in practice. The pursuit of excellence is a process by which each individual appreciates for himself the nature of the tasks he has to perform and the disciplines that are required, and absorbs these into his own perception and performance while at the same time adding something of his own. There is a challenge and meeting this challenge requires not just effort and endurance, but also imagination and inspiration, and in the end selflessness; the pursuit of excellence is a process of extending human capabilities towards their fullest potential and thus of getting closer to God.

These various aspects of what motivates people in their paid employment may be summarised as follows. First there is the extent to which working, working effectively and pursuing excellence are an intrinsic part of human nature, with the implication that if a contract of employment did not provide a context for putting them into practice an alternative context would need to be found. Then there is an acquisitive element, of working in order to acquire money, status and power for their own sakes. The pursit of these goals is different from the pursuit of excellence since money, status and power are all human inventions and when acquired tend not to satisfy, whereas excellence is something external to humanity and God-given. And finally there is the pursuit of money, status and power as a means to something else, which may or may not be satisfying. Money may be spent on bringing up a family or on the pursuit of some self-fulfilling interest, or it may be spent on self-defeating self-indulgence. Status and power may be used as an opportunity for sorting out some of the mess that the world is in and thus for enabling a little bit more of God's will to happen than would have happened otherwise, or agian it may be used for self-defeating self-indulgence that may damage other people and make it that much harder for everybody to be the selves that God would wish.

And now what of love? It was into a world that was well used to work, and thoroughly familiar with all the various motivations for it, that Jesus was born, and what he showed, both in his teaching and by his example, was a motivation different from all of them. He showed the love of God for man, and man's capability for opening himself up to this love. God's love is given to everybody by virtue of their being his creations, and is not dependant upon any attempt to win his favour, or upon merit measured in terms of a commitment to a set of defined values, or upon achievement measured in terms of the effective performance of defined tasks. Insofar as a person is aware of being loved by God, this evokes a response in him which is to return this love. This happens not so much through effort as through surrender; the more completely a person surrenders himself to God's love, the more complete will be the love that he returns. Man's surrender to God's love will also manifest itself in love for other people and for the created world, once again not so much as a result of any effort made to imitate God's love but by means of God's love flowing through him and on to others. This love by man for others is also unrelated to any merit or achievement, since others are the object of his love merely by virtue of being God's creations too. This love is essentially empathetic in that it takes the form of each person sharing in other people's experiences and of God sharing in everybody's; God's purpose for each one of us is that we should do his will and express our true potential, and there is joy when God's will happens and pain when it doesn't. The New Testament word for this love is *agape*, and many subsequent Christian writers have used this Greek word when describing it. An awareness of it is evident throughout the Gospels, and it is systematically described by St Paul, most comprehensively in I Corinthians chapter 13.

It is certainly wrong to see *agape* as a Christian invention, since God's love for his people and their capacity to receive it and respond to it existed from the beginning of time; it merely became more understandable by virtue of Jesus' example. It is also wrong to see it as a Christian discovery; there is ample evidence of an awareness of it in the Old Testament, particularly in the Book of Job and in Second Isaiah, and it is discernable also in classical Greek literature, particularly in some of the less Platonic attitudes of Socrates, and in the drama most obviously in Oedipus at Colonnus. However once Jesus' life, death and resurrection has been witnessed and recorded, his awareness of God's love became a significant factor in humanity's perception of itself and in the future course of historical events.

So what is the nature of the obligations to which a person who is aware of God's love is subjected? An awareness of this love leads to a realisation that true self-hood requires a total surrender of the self so that it becomes inbued with wonder at the immensity of the purpose in creation and at the extent of the love of which this purpose consists. This surrender leads to a closer relationship with God and to a fuller understanding of the nature of his will and of how things ought to be if true potential is to be achieved. It also leads to a desire to put God's will into practice since denying it causes pain; denying it means that a person is cutting himself off from God's love and once experienced the deprivation of it hurts. Then there is the obligation to allow this love to flow through the self and onwards to other people and to the whole of creation. At this stage love is an attitude rather than a series of actions, but it is an attitude which is clearly visible to third parties who can see, if they know how to recognise it, a self that is at peace and which is close to the achievement of its true potential as a result of it having been, at least in part, denied and subsumed within its origin. And finally there is the obligation to translate this love into action by becoming an agent through whom God's will is done and others are assisted in the achievement of their true potential too. These are the obligations, and the motivation is simple and straight forward. An awareness of God's love carries with it a desire to behave in the way that this awareness implies. The fact that the motivation is simple and straight forward doesn't mean that being guided by it is simple and straight forward; being human means that there is always plenty of scope for distortions and distractions to get in the way.

So how do the obligations and the motivations that relate to employment and to love compare? The first point is that such obligations as an awareness of God's love implies are different in kind from the obligations consequent upon a contract of employment. When a person enters into a contract of employment, he undertakes to do a number of predefined things and so long as he does them he receives a number of predefined benefits. A person's relationship with God, on the other hand, is not contractual since God's love is always there for the asking and a person may avail himself of its benefits insofar as he chooses to or is able to, simply by making himself open to it. The performance of institutionally defined tasks is a contractual requirement, whereas actions that are motivated by love are undertaken voluntarily. Loving is a motivation which finds its expression in a freely taken decision to put God's will for others first, and this is what characterises it rather than any helpful consequences that may result. Institutional tasks may also have helpful consequences but what matters is that the institution requires that they be performed. An employee may well find that the performance of his institutional tasks provides him with opportunities for expressing love towards other people or towards the created world, but insofar as this happens it is outside the institution's concern; loving is not something that an institution has any right to demand of its employees, and Section 57 of the Employment Protection (Consolidation) Act does not allow a shortfall in loving as grounds for fair dismissal.

If a person goes in to look after a bed-ridden neighbour, this is love, but when a district nurse goes in to look after him she is performing a task that she is contracted to perform and would be in breach of contact is she didn't go in. In practical terms, the district nurse's contribution is likely to be the more helpful because it is probable that she will have a greater professional competence, and it is also possible that the bed-ridden person may feel more loved by the district nurse, but what matters is that the first person gave up something that was his, in this case time, in order to help somebody else. The same is true if a person gives an unemployed neighbour £5 of his own money; this is love even if it is less helpful and less appreciated than the £25 handed over by the DHSS desk clerk as one of the tasks he is contracted to perform. And a person who tills hs backgarden on a Saturday afternoon is reflecting God's love for the natural world whereas a municipally employed gardener tilling a park is doing it because the District Council has told him to; he is not sacrificing his time or money since the District Council is actually paying him to be there. At this stage, it may look as though Christian district nurses, DHSS desk clerks and municipal gardeners are under no Christian obligation while about their paid employment other than to perform their appointed tasks to the best of their ability, but the crucial question of how they, and indeed all Christians who are subject to a contract of employment, do in fact express the love towards other people and the created world that their knowledge of God's love will cause them to feel is addressed in Chapter 7. The point that is made here is merely that contractual obligations and the obligations of love are different in kind.

The second point about the differences between the obligations of employment and the obligations of love is that contractual obligations are ultimately rejecting whereas God's love is ultimately accepting. The performance of institutionally defined tasks is a contractual requirement, and their non-performance is a breach of contract which will result ultimately in the contract being withdrawn. Actions that are motivated by love, on the other hand, are undertaken as a consequence of the presence of that love, and their non-performance results only in an awareness of that love having been denied. The knowledge of failure is likely to be painful in both cases, but whereas the only recourse open to a sacked employee who wishes to reestablish a relationship with the institution is to seek a new contract of employment which may or may not be offered, God's love is never withdrawn; the pain felt by a sinner is an aspect of repentance and is made worse by the knowledge of God's continuing concern. When an employee is sacked, the institution loses his services, but this on balance must be an advantage to the institution since otherwise it wouldn't have sacked him; he may be difficult to replace, but this is a specific recruitment problem, and though there may be one or two colleagues who are sorry to see him go, the institution itself is capable of neither sadness nor remorse. God, on the other hand, because of his vision of the perfectability of each individual person and because of his empathy with all human feelings, suffers at every instance of a person falling short but does not reject even the most hardened of sinners.

A third point is that contracts of employment do not affect the employee as a whole person. An employee contracts to make available to an institution a limited proportion of his time and energy, and to undertake a limited number and range of tasks. With one or two exceptions, the institution has no interest in what an employee does when he is off duty, and should not attempt to influence him unduly. The exceptions are to do with the risk that certain forms of behaviour, even if they occur outside working hours, may bring the institution into disrepute, and with the continuing obligations on people like doctors and policemen whose institutional role extends beyond clocking-off time. And for many people it is out of working hours that they are most truly themselves, when they are with their families and friends or pursuing their individual interests.

The love of God, on the other hand, is all-pervasive and people who are aware of it will feel a need to reflect it and respond to it at all times both during and outside working hours. During working hours there will inevitably be some conflict with contractual requirements, but there is scope for loving nonetheless and how this can be managed is explored in Chapter 7. If God's love is seen as sufficiently all-embracing as to include workplaces and all that goes on in them, many of the tensions will disappear and work will be seen as offering scope both for worship and for self-fulfilment through doing his will.

6

Distinction Four:
Redemption and Institutional Reform

Everybody irrespective of the degree of their religious commitment would agree that things in this world are far from perfect, and this chapter looks at the world's imperfections and at the processes for putting them right. The distinction which it makes is between human imperfection, where putting things right is a matter of repentance and redemption through God's grace, and institutional imperfection, where putting things right is a matter of institutional reform, a process undertaken by human beings in the full knowledge of their limited intelligence and partial experience.

Chapter 4 made the point that human beings and institutions are different in kind. Both are capable of falling short of their full potential, and this imperfection causes damage both to the person or institution concerned and also to other people and institutions with whom they may be connected. The Christian word for imperfection in people is sin, and the most helpful view of sin is to see it in terms of the literal meaning of the New Testament word *harmartia*, which means missing the mark or falling short of whatever it is that God intends us to be. The alternative view is to see sin as a breach of some defined code of attitude or behaviour, but this raises enormous difficulties as to what any such code should comprise and what authority it should carry, and in any event thinking in terms of the breaching of defined rules is an institutional approach which seem ill-equipped to take proper account of the differeing predicaments of individual people.

God knows our potential as individuals, and is therefore aware of every extent to which we fall short. No doubt such shortcomings cause him sadness, but his love for us continues in the sense that he does not reject us on account of our failure and the opportunity for making things good is always there whether or not we are willing or able to make use of it. The prerequisite for making things good is repentance, which means being honest with ourselves first about the fact of the shortfall and then about its nature and the reasons for it. This awareness is inevitably painful, and the pain may either cause us to erect defences against it which act as a barrier to God's love and thus postpone the process of making good, or it may provide us with an incentive to remove the barriers in the full knowledge that God continues to find us acceptable. This openness to God is redemption, and it enables us to learn more from him about what our true potential is and about the nature of his will. This expanded vision of our potential turns the initial shortcomings to good account so that they become relevant not as instances of failure but as opportunities for improvement, and this is absolution.

God's purpose is to ensure that his will is done by means of each individual person achieving his full potential as a human being. The purpose of an institution, on the other hand, is to ensure that its objectives are met, and this means that what it requires of its staff is that they perform their allocated tasks competently. It is interested in their personal shortcomings only insofar as they affect work performance, which means that much of human sinfulness is outside its concern. Some personal shortcomings, nevertheless, do affect a person's work performance, for example if he is so sensitive about his weight that he loses his temper with his colleagues whenever he thinks that a reference has been made to it, or if he is so shy that he is unable to make his voice heard at meetings. Shortcomings such as these are susceptible either to the sort of work-based remedies that are discussed later, or to the processes of repentance and redemption since they are the sort of difficulties that may be alleviated by increasing self-knowledge and self-confidence. God's offer of redemption is always available, within the workplace as well as outside it.

Since institutions are concerned solely with getting the work done, their attitude towards their staff will be very different from God's. Institutions are interested in aptitudes, skills, and experience. Aptitudes are the characteristics that people are born with, such as their potential for being good at mathematics. God loves a person irrespective of how good he is at mathematics and continues to love him even if he is hopeless, but a person's mathematical ability will be a significant factor in whether or not an institution wishes to employ him. Skills are what people acquire as a result of training and experience, like being able to work out degrees of significance in statistical variables. God would no doubt be quite pleased that a person had succeeded in developing his aptitude to the extent of being able to do this, but for an institution considering him for a particular post it might be crucial. And experience means having learned what matters and what doesn't and what works best, like knowing that data from one source is likely to be more accurate than data from another and knowing how particular findings may be presented most effectively. Once again, God is probably pleased that a person has been able to develop his aptitudes and to learn, but what matters to his employing institution is that he is capable of making a particular presentation accurately, quickly and effectively.

Institutions make use of a number of procedures to ensure that the staff they employ do the work that is required of them to the required standard, for example selection, training, and the imposition of disciplinary sanctions. Selection is used to ensure that staff are recruited who have the appropriate aptitudes, and that they are placed in positions appropriate to the skills and experience. Wherever there is a serious mismatch, staff will need to be transferred or dismissed if their performance is inadequate, and transferred or promoted if their performance is unnecessarily good. Training is used in order to ensure that staff develop the skills that are appropriate for the tasks that they are required to perform; career development is also a form of training which is used to ensure that staff acquire an appropriate range of experience. And disciplinary procedures are necessary both in order to protect the institution from behaviour that is likely to jeopardise the achievement of its objectives and in order to enforce the appropriate ethical standards which it is in the institution's interest to promote. These procedures are different from God's in a number of important ways. Institutional procedures are related to the achievement of objectives which have been defined by people and which are therefore capable of being understood by people. They are also operated by people who, even if they shut themselves behind boardroom doors, are nonetheless sufficiently visible for it to be

63

certain that they are human and therefore fallible. This means that, however odd these procedures may appear, they are in no sense mysterious and do not deserve to be treated with reverence or awe. A further difference is that they have only a partial application since they relate only to those aspects of people that are relevant to the performance of their institutional tasks, whereas God is concerned with the whole person. But the most important difference is that they are ultimately rejecting in that they are operated with dismissal as the final sanction whereas God, because his love always continues, is ultimately accepting.

However this chapter is concerned not only with the shortcomings of the people who work in institutions but also the shortcomings of institutions themselves. Just as people are incapable of total openness to God, so institutions often fall short of perfect performance, and just as the shortcomings of people are capable of causing damage to others, so the shortcomings of institutions are capable of causing damage often on a proportionally larger scale.

Some of the shortcomings of institutions are the result of inadequacies in their organisational structure, for example in their procedures for the recruitment, deployment and disciplining of staff; although institutions are not synonymous with the staff they employ, the staff they employ do represent a significant component. In a successful institution, the institution's organisational structure will have within itself means of identifying and remedying its own inadequacies; a responsibility for monitoring performance against objectives will be built into people's job descriptions at all levels and there will be a whole range of internal review procedures, staff suggestion schemes, and joint consultation arrangements. Joint consultation often involves trade union representatives, and provides an opportunity for bringing organisational shortcomings and grievances to the attention of management and a mechanism for arriving at an agreed view on what organisational changes are necessary and how they might best be implemented. This is constructive trade union involvement, but it has to be said that there are also instances where trade unions have resisted organisational change with consequences that have been destructive in the longer term.

Organisational change is a process implemented entirely by

human beings. It is misleading and unhelpful to make parallels between repentance and the indentification of institutional shortcomings, or between redemption and the process of implementing institutional change, or between absolution and successfully implemented change being reflected in improved institutional performance. God's forgiving love is nowhere apparent in organisational change, and there is no element of grace; the processes are initiated by people and implemented by people with a variety of intentions and with limited knowledge and abilities. I know a Christian management consultant who used to pray before each assignment "Thy will be done", but he found this an inappropriate prayer because he was reluctant to identify God's will with the eventual outcome. He now asks for a blessing on the management consultancy skills that God has endowed him with.

There is, however, a more complex area of institutional inadequacy. An institution will not be successful unless its tasks are properly related to its objectives, its objectives to its purpose, and its purpose to the needs that it was set up to meet; the relationship between tasks, objectives, purpose and needs ought to be kept constantly under review because there is a constant need for realignment. The questions that need to be asked are, first, what are the created world's unmet needs? Then, how can these needs best be met? Then, what needs to be done in order to meet them in this way? And then, what does this mean in terms of actual work? A misconceived answer to any one of these questions will result in institutional malfunction which may in turn lead to damage to the created world and to human suffering.

If a washing machine factory loses sight of the fact that its purpose is to produce washing machines that people will actually buy, it may find itself turning out over-priced machines which don't sell, which will mean that it will go bankrupt and its shareholders will lose their money and its staff their jobs. If it fails to appreciate the relevance of microchips to programme selection, its potential customers will buy other machines which are more flexible in how they wash, so that its market share will decline and bankruptcy again may follow. A school needs to be constantly aware of its obligation to educate its children in preparation for the lives they will acutually lead, and this requires a constant rejigging of the balance between the skills and understanding which the children are offered, and maintaining the essential core of the educational process. If microchips are to be a feature of life in the future, children need to know what microchips can do and how to use them or else they will be ill-equipped in the competition for jobs. On the other hand if microcomputing is taught at the expense of giving the children a sense of their own nature and value as individuals, they will end up uneducated in a more basic sense; school is one of the places where children are prepared for the responsibilities of adulthood, and if this sense of responsibility is not acqured the natural world and the other people in it will be placed at risk. And the criminal courts need to keep sight of their obligations in the maintenance of a safe and just society, and this requires reducing the risk of criminals being acquitted on technicalities, constantly reassessing the nature and the relative harmfulness of different types of offending, and reviewing the effects and effectiveness of different types of criminal sanctions; it is harmful for society if, say, shop-lifting is punished more severely than company fraud, or if certain offenders have to be given potentially damaging prison sentences because the facilities for non-custodial alternatives are not available.

There are a number of mechanisms that help to ensure that institutional purposes, objectives and tasks are kept in correct alignment with each other and in proper relationship with the needs that the institution was set up to meet. The first is through the internal procedures already referred to; one of an institution's primary responsibilities is to ensure its own survival and continuing relevance, and to wind itself up if this can't be managed. There is a contractual obligation on all members of an institution's staff to ask themselves the questions that are relevant to this responsibility and to come up with the best answers they can. Nevertheless, institutions sometimes fail in the exercise of this responsibility, sometimes because of innate inertia, and sometimes because of the vested interest that most employees have in the perpetuation of things as they are; staff understandably wish to retain their jobs and to continue to use the skills they have already acquired to maintain their institutional role, status and power. And also there are sometimes instances where the employees of an institution do not have the necessary abilities to exercise this responsibility, and instances where whatever their level of ability they get things inadvertantly wrong.

The second mechanism is throught the corrective processes that were described in Chapter 4, market forces in the case of commercial institutions, and political scrutiny and the democratic process in the case of representative institutions. If a washing machine factory fails to produce the right sort of machine at the right price, customers will not buy them, the factory will cease to be commercially viable, and it will disappear into the hands of the receiver. If the executive of a tenants' association or a trade union, or indeed if a Government, fails to do what its electorate wishes or does what its electorate doesn't wish, there is a mechanism for it to be voted out of office at the next opportunity so that the processes of ensuring correct alignment and relevance can start afresh. However even these corrective processes cannot always be relied upon to be universally effective. Once again there is the factor of innate inertia, particularly in the political field since politicians are often reluctant to intervene until the need for intervention is popularly apparent which may be after the damage has been done. There is also the possibility of the procedures being manipulated, particularly within representative institutions where there is often scope for the people who have been elected to office to conceal their actions from those they are answerable to. And there is also the possibility of cross-connivance, for example where politicians decide to inject public money into a failing commercial institution in order to distort the effect of market forces, which may or may not be justified by longer term considerations.

As well as there being a need to ensure the continuing relevance of existing institutions and the correct alignment of their tasks, objectives, purposes and needs, there is also the inevitability of new needs being perceived and new ways of meeting old needs being appreciated. Not many years ago there were no washing machine factories because no one at that stage had realised that machines might be made that were capable of meeting people's clothes-washing needs. And there is also the ever-present possibility that corrective intervention will be prevented because of gaps in the existing institutional framework. An example of a recently created institution is the Office'of the Health Service Commissioner which was set up following the realisation that there were no adequate procedures for investigating complaints of maladministration in the NHS.

Where the internal procedures of institutions have failed to prevent institutional malfunction, and where remedial action has not been triggered by the corrective commercial or democratic procedures, there remains a third process by which institutional reform can be brought about. This is through the initiative of individual people who are aware of the damage that may be or is being done, acting either singly or in groups. It is different from the two processes already described in that the first two either happen or fail to happen of their own accord, or they happen or fail to happen as a result of people in their institutional capacity performing their required institutional tasks. This third process is dependant upon individuals exercising their personal judgement and making use of their freedom to do what they personally think is for the best. The obvious people to initiate such action are those who are at the receiving end of the damage, but they are not always in a position to do so, perhaps because the damage done to them is so great that they are incapacitated, or perhaps because the very reason why they have become the victims of institutional damage is because the relevant institutions are not equipped to take account of their interests anyway. An example of the former is patients who have suffered brain damage as a result of using a particular prescribed drug. And perhaps the most celebrated recent example of the latter is the black people who were disenfranchised by the electoral systems in a number of southern states in America and who were unable to use their political influence to improve their position in society because of their very disenfranchisement; they needed the assistance of other people, and when this assistance came in 1963 the process of institutional reform began. People who feel themselves to be the victims of institutional shortcomings need not assume that because the institution ignores their needs they should not attempt to initiate institutional reform, and there is plenty of scope for people who are not victims taking action to initiate institutional reform on behalf of people who are.

The scope for this sort of individual or group action is

enormous. It ranges from the monitoring of individual institutions at local level to the demonstration of concern about all that is wrong with the created world. There are so many wrongs that Christians and non-Christians alike would like to see righted, resources inequitably allocated, people malnourished and dying of starvation, people inadequately educated, housed or cared for, people whose rights are infringed or who are the victims of violence. Insofar as there is opportunity for righting these wrongs on the scale that is needed, it can only be through improving the functioning of institutions, institutions like the UN and its agencies, the International Monetary Fund and the World Bank, the multi-national corporations and the political institutions of individual countries. There is in fact so much scope for institutional reform, and so much good that would come of it if it were actually to happen, that Christians need to consider very carefully the difficult question of the nature of such obligations as they may be under to involve themselves in seeking to bring it about.

Contemporary Christian thinking on this question is divided. There is one perspective, encapsulated in Dr Edward Norman's 1978 Reith Lectures which were later published under the title *Christianity and the World Order*, and another perspective which has as its extreme expression the Liberation theology of Gustavo Guttierez and Leonardo Boff and which is encapsulated in more restrained Anglican form in Bishop David Shepherd's book *Bias to the Poor*. The Norman view, essentially, is that the concern of religion is with individual and corporate spirituality and that the secular world is merely the environment within which such spirituality happens; improvements in the material lot of deprived people, though desirable, can only be implemented by technical and political means which are appropriately evaluated against technical and political rather than spiritual criteria. The Shepherd view, in contrast, is that improving the material lot of deprived people by whatever means is a central matter of Christian concern and that Christians are directly obliged to contribute to this improvement as best they are able including by technical and political means. Both quote the passage from Isaiah which Jesus recites in the synagogue in St Luke chapter 4,

He has sent me to announce good news to the poor,
To proclaim release for prisoners and recovery of sight for the blind;

To let the broken victims go free,
To proclaim the year of the Lord's favour,

but Norman sees it as a message of salvation for individuals and Shepherd as an imperative for corporate action.

The difficulty with the Norman view is that it would seem to limit the area of Christian concern. A Christian cannot help but share, at least to some extent, God's concern for his world and the people who inhabit it, and will be inspired by his vision of the Kingdom to desire that society be organised in such a way as to ensure that the created world is properly respected and the scope for the realisation of human potential maximised. This is an important part of the responsibility laid upon man for making order out of chaos and for cultivating the earth and making it fruitful, and since institutional shortcomings are often a significant impediment to the implementation of God's will, it means that concern about institutional shortcomings is a proper concern for Christian people. In the Old Testament, particularly in the Pentateuch, the worship of God, a concern for the world and all its people, and the way in which society is organised, are all intimately linked, and although there is little direct reference to this linkage in the New Testament it seems probable that Jesus and the New Testament writers took it for granted.

This means that there is a responsibility laid upon humanity to devise and implement social arrangements that are as effective as possible in ensuring respect for the world and the maximisation of the scope for the fulfilment of human potential. However, since human beings are flawed and of limited intelligence and imagination, the effectiveness of the arrangements that man is capable of devising will inevitably be limited too. And since institutions are the creation of flawed and limited human beings, institutional arrangements will be of limited effectiveness also. This means that there is always scope for institutional arrangements to be improved, but equally it means that changes which are humanly implemented will not necessarily be for the better. The difficulty with the Shepherd view is the risk that, if attempts at institutional reform are judged solely in terms of the quality of the motivation that inspired them, there can be no guarantee that social benefits will actually result. Attempts to bring about change need to be judged first by the extent to which the attempts actually succeed, and then by

70

the extent to which the change has beneficial results, particularly insofar as spiritual benefits result from the improvements.

The main problem is that a desire to see the world properly respected and the scope for the realisation of human potential maximised is a very broad-brush aspiration which does not contain within itself any indication as to the means by which the desire may best be translated into effective action. Although responsibility for caring for the world and its people, for making order out of chaos and for cultivating the earth and making it fruitful, is laid by God upon humanity, the means by which this responsibility is discharged and the ways in which the caring actually happens are and can only be through the application of human effort, intelligence and imagination. A few miracles and instances of divine intervention apart, which in any case should not be generalised from, the way in which God's will is implemented is through human beings with all their limitations doing the best they can. It is unhelpful and almost certainly misleading to think that any single method of caring carries any particular divine imprint or is authenticated by divine imprint when compared with any other method. The Pentateuch does give divine imprint to certain aspects of human behaviour and to certain elements of social organisation, and this causes problems nowadays for a number of fundamentalist Christians since some of these requirements, however desirable they may have been in their time, have become totally unrealistic and often meaningless in the world of today. Nevertheless it is possible to derive from the Pentateuch an awareness of the need to control behaviour and to arrange society in a way that reflects a proper concern for the world and its people, and this remains a relevant source of inspiration alongside inspiration from other sources.

An important part of the way in which God's will for the world is brought about is through people working effectively in the course of their institutional employment. Insofar as institutions are perpetrating damage or are being only partially effective, institutions need to be reformed. Looked at in terms of the subjective view of work, an important part of each person's self-fulfilment is seeking to achieve institutional reform so that more of God's will for the world is done. Looked at in terms of the objective view of work, what matters is a reformed institution at the end of the day, and institutional reform requires the effective application of aptitudes, skill and experience; naive concern is not enough. This is what Archbishop Temple had in mind when he talked of the autonomy of technique. There is a story that he was once about to go into hospital for an operation and was asked if he was insisting upon being operated on by a Christian surgeon, to which he replied that what he was insisting upon was that he be operated on by a good surgeon. There are areas where it is inappropriate to apply criteria that are Christian only in the narrowest sense.

All this puts both the Church and individual Christians who would speak in God's name in a somewhat negative position. There is a clear Christian responsibility to criticise those aspects of social arrangements which cause damage to the earth or its people, or which put certain people at a disadvantage when compared with other people, and there is a clear justification in saying that such damage, deprivation or discrimination is contrary to God's will. On the other hand there is no clear locus in identifying God's will with any particular course of remedial action. As the body of Christ, the Church's task is to present God's will to man, and there is a real risk that its task will be compromised and that its presentation of God's will will lose credibility if the Church identifies itself too readily with a particular course of action that is no more than the outcome of the exercise of man's limited intelligence and partial experience. It is appropriate that the Church should proclaim the damage caused to individual people by unemployment, and also that it should proclaim the damage caused by inflation, but the former does not mean that it should necessarily identify God's will with reflationary policies of the latter with deflationary ones.

Nevertheless individual Christians, including individual clergy, will often feel that one particular policy is to be preferred to another on the grounds that its implementation will lead to a closer approximation of the Kingdom being realised, and pressure is frequently put upon the Church, both nationally and locally, to associate itself with particular causes or issues. These situations need to be looked at very carefully whenever they arise. The motivation behind the pressure needs to be carefully assessed since there is always the possibility that it arises from its proponents' need for divine authentication for their cause or from their need to visit divine disapproval on the causes of their opponents, perhaps because they are too naive or bigotted to see the merits of their opponents' causes or the demerits of their own. Even where the motivation is not suspect in this way, there is still the need for a very careful assessment of whether there is a risk of trespassing on the autonomy of technique. Even where the Church has access to people with tried and tested technical expertise it is very risky to identify God's will with their particular expertise rather than with the expertise of others; technical expertise is a gift bestowed by God on a great many people and not only on people who are prepared to make it available to the Church. And there is always the risk that the Church, in identifying itself with one particular side of any social debate, will alienate the proponents of the other side who may nonetheless be in need of what the Church more generally has to offer.

It is important that a clear distinction be drawn between specific attempts to change the objectives and the workings of particular institutions on the one hand, and the proclaiming of the shortcomings and injustices inherent in society on the other, whether they be within individual people or within the institutions that people have created. Both have honourable places within the Christian tradition, but the more clearly the distinction is drawn the better for all concerned. The motivation behind the proclamation of injustice is that instances of God's will not being done need to be shouted about so that God's will as a dimension in individual behaviour and in the organisation of society doesn't get forgotten. This sort of shouting is what the Old Testament prophets did, and its present day equivalent is often referred to as the exercise of the prophetic role. However it is not at all clear that prophets like Amos, Isaiah of Jerusalem or Jeremiah, in drawing public attention to the shortcomings of their society and of its institutions, were actually trying to change the way that their society and institutions worked. If they were, they were singularly unsuccessful and would have been better advised to have set about the task in some other way. What they were concerned to do was to ensure that God's will as a factor capable of influencing social organisation and political decision-making was kept within the public consciousness, and that people were made aware that the inevitable result of disregarding God's will was social damage. They were also, particularly Hosea, concerned with proclaiming the fact, that in spite of all this backsliding and in spite of the damage, God's love for his people continued.

The distinction between institutional reform and prophetic proclamation becomes blurred where objectives are deferred. In drawing attention to aspects of social arrangements that are socially divisive or damaging, Christians may be attempting not so much to persuade specific institutions to implement immediate reforms as to influence the climate of public opinion so that the implementation of reforms becomes more likely at some future date. Where this is the intention, the initiative needs to be defined as institutional reform and judged in terms of its long-term beneficial impact. However there are a number of instances where specific policy objectives are pursued for reasons that are more prophetic than reformist, and unilateral nuclear disarmament is an obvious example. Christians have obvious reasons for preferring peace ot nuclear war, and campaigning for unilateral nuclear disarmament is an obvious way of demonstrating this preference in a prophetic way. However the campaign is rarely presented in a form that seems designed to make implementation likely, and the consequences of implementation are rarely thought through. It would be much more straightforward if the campaign were pursued in a way that emphasised its prophetic nature rather in a way that created the impression that the purpose was to influence policy.

All this said, it is institutional reform that this chapter is about. Attempts to achieve it need to be judged in terms of their actual beneficial effect, and success requires the application of a great deal of knowledge and skill. It is necessary to know what procedures to use and which to ignore, who to approach and at what time, and how to present a case in the way that is most likely to be effective. It involves negotiation, bulldozing and compromise, and these require a knowledge of how to use power. Above all, institutional reform requires that an accurate assessment be made of how far it is possible to go. Institutions are fragile; most institutions do a great deal of good and some harm, and too much change implemented too quickly can have the effect of diminishing the good or even of destroying the institution altogether. And, particularly in the case of large institutions, there is a limit to the amount of change that can be absorbed at any given time. An institution's response to pressure for too much change is likely to be a battening down of the hatches in self-defence. When Cleopatra was confronted with news she was incapable of absorbing, her reaction was to have the messenger whipped. Institutions have at their disposal a variety of ways of whipping unwelcome messengers, most obviously by discrediting them, and since any message from a discredited messenger is by definition the wrong message, an institution's reaction to pressure for too much reform is likely to be for it to move stubbornly in the opposite direction.

Something needs to be said about the special position of would-be reformers who are in the employ of the institution that they wish to reform. These people need to remember the obligations and the constraints on their freedom of action that have accepted in agreeing to be bound by their contracts of employment. Most institutions have internal procedures for considering suggestions for reform and the proper course, at least initially, is for a would-be reformer to use these. There is usually consultative machinery which enables suggestions from individuals to be considered, and there are also formal and informal methods of influencing line management or for making representation to shareholders, Management Committees, Boards of Directors, Boards of Governors or whoever. Where the use of internal procedures fails to result in the desired reform, the employee may choose to accept this as an indication that the cumulative wisdom of the institution is greater than his maybe naive individual vision, or he may decide to pursue his campaign further, for example by resort to devices that may make him liable to disciplinary action such as speaking at public meetings or leaking information to the press. Whether or not he does these this is a matter for his judgement, but he needs to remember that he is bound by his contract of employment and that if he chooses to act in breach of its conditions he is obliged to accept the consequences even to the point of accepting dismissal. He has no right to criticise his employing institution for exercising its part of a contractual agreement however much he may feel that his actions were justified.

In distinguishing between redemption and institutional reform, it is important not to lose sight of the extent to which people's scope for personal fulfilment is dependant upon the institutional arrangements which govern the society in which they happen to live. Man fulfils himself by reflecting God's love and by doing God's will, and this response takes place at a number of different levels. At its most basic, the response takes the form merely of surviving since life itself is an affirmation of God. Death is eventualy inevitable, but nevertheless there is scope for social policy to reflect God's will in prolonging lives and in preventing premature deaths. One level up, people's response takes the form of working to ensure that the earth continues to prosper and give of its goodness for the benefit of all, and social policies can certainly increase the scope for productive and effective working. One level up from this, the response takes the form of people making good use of their creativity, their imagination and their intelligence so that they may express to the full the abilities that God has endowed them with. The scope for social policy to affect this is somewhat less direct, since creativity, imagination and intelligence are capable of being applied to whatever circumstances may prevail, but social policy is relevant in that in times of social disorder their application is constantly interrupted, and in a divided society some people are presented with more scope for applying their abilities than others. However the most important response by people to the love of God is through loving, and the exercise of loving is totally irrespective of social conditions and of any influence that social policy may exert. One of the indisputable facts about sacrificial love is that it is capable of blossoming in circumstances where social justice is most manifestly absent, for example in concentration camps, in refugee camps, and in the most deprived communities. Love is a response to people whatever and however great their needs; indeed the greater and more obvious the needs the more obvious is the scope for loving. And also love has a tendency to slip out of the spectrum of social relationships when deprivations are eased and when the domination of some people by others is lessened. The implementation of policies embodying social justice should remain an ambition of Christian people even though when such policies are effectively established the need for love may become less apparent and human aspirations may tend to be expressed in material terms or in terms of relative status.

The ideal which social policies aim to embody is social justice, which is a vision of social arrangements within which all people are treated fairly and as being of equal value, and this is a proper inspiration for Christians. The vision is in some ways comparable to the Marxist vision of the socialist society, but this is no argument for identifying Marxism with Christianity or the socialist society with the Kingdom of God. The Kingdom of God is characterised by the unimpeded expression of love, and social justice can be assumed to follow from such a state of affairs. The vision of the socialist state, on the other hand, assumes the achievement of social justice by means of the perfecting of institutions and assumes that the perfecting of individuals and of their relationships with each other will follow from this. In making these assumptions it takes no account of sin. Christianity sees sin as the impediment to the coming of the Kingdom, whereas Marxism sees the impediment to the coming of the socialist society in terms of shortcomings in social arrangements and in particular in terms of the shortcomings of institutions. Both agree on the desirability of improved social arrangements, but Christians see a prior and paramount need for individual redemption.

I was once told a revised version of the parable of the Good Samaritan. When the Samaritan saw the traveller beaten and abandoned at the side of the road, he came to the conclusion that his most effective response would be to leave him there to die since the publicity that his death would inevitably attract would force the police into improving patrolling of the highway which would reduce the likelihood of future travellers being set upon. The point that was being made was that if the Samaritan had been genuinely concerned with redemption he would have behaved as in St Luke chapter 10, but if his preoccupation had been with institutional reform he might well have concluded that it was expedient that one man should die for the people, and this rational assessment of the situation might well have constrained his compassionate response to a fellow human being in need. This is an unfair story in that it manipulates the context in order to imply that institutional reform is somehow evil rather than something very worthwhile that millions of employees are engaged in every day, but nevertheless it does illustrate very vividly the difference between institutional reform and individual redemption. Institutional reform and individual redemption both enable changes to happen for the better; the difference between them is that people are capable of being redeemed directly by God whereas institutions can only be reformed by people inspired by their vision of the Kingdom using their God-given skills.

7

Integration One: The Individual in the Workplace

This chapter returns to the task of suggesting a framework within which an individual employee might be able to experience his paid employment as an important aspect of his response to God rather than as something totally separated from God's concern, and in so doing it takes into account the distinctions made in the previous four chapters. The basic components of such a framework have already been established. Chaos needs to be transformed into order and the earth needs to be cultivated and made fruitful, and each individual person needs to feel that he is making his own particular contribution to these tasks. The work that he does in the course of his paid employment is an important aspect of his contribution, and if he is able to see it as such he will feel that he is participating in however small a way in humanity's response to God's charge. And at the same time man needs to spend at least some of his time working and applying his intelligence and his creativity to his work; this is part of God's will for each individual person and paid employment provides each individual employee with an opportunity for putting it into practice.

This is the bare skeleton of the framework but two difficulties remain which this chapter addresses. The first is how, given that insofar as people are aware of being loved by God they will feel a need to reflect that love at all times including during working hours, they can find adequate scope for the expression of love in the workplace. And the second is how a person's response to those inevitable occasions when his employing institution does damage to the world and its people instead of helping them can be consistent with his awareness of God's love. Chapter 5 made the important point that whatever an employee might be motivated to do in the way of expressing God's love during working hours, the requirements of his contract of employment are paramount and take precedence over everything else. There is no way in which an employee has any right to expect the institution to which he is contracted to release him from his contractual obligations on grounds of his Christian commitment, or indeed on any other grounds. And Chapter 5 also made the point that an institution has the right to demand from its employees a significant degree of personal loyalty and commitment including on those occasions when the institution does what the employee might consider to be the wrong thing; there is clearly a limit to the extent of this loyalty and commitment and Chapter 6 looked at how situations can be coped with when that loyalty and commitment are severely strained. Nevertheless there are problems inherent in the miriad of compromises, frustrations and sadnesses that work demands of us daily which have to be capable of resolution within any integrated framework that is likely to be of genuine help.

The scope for the expression of God's love in the workplace is thus limited to what is possible within the parameters set by the primacy of institutional requirements, but luckily there are withing these parameters three kinds of opportunity. The first kind results from institutional requirements being somewhat less than monolithic; there are interstices between institutional commitments within which personal relationships with colleagues and others can be formed which are capable of being developed into loving relationships. Within even the most clock-watching of institutions there are coffee-breaks and lunch-breaks and many other sorts of breaks between bouts of work activity and these can provide ample opportunity for employees to get to know one another as people. The very act of working together can create a strong personal bond, and these bonds often mature into valuable personal relationships which may perhaps be continued outside working hours. Nevertheless, getting the work done remains the top priority, and time spent talking with colleagues has to be made up either by longer hours or by more intensive work.

The second kind of opportunity results from the fact that, even though institutional requirements have to be met, a certain amount of flexibility is permitted in the way that they are met. A manager's contractual obligation is to manage his staff, but withing this obligation he can manage his staff compassionately as well as managing them efficiently; management can be supplemented with love. Many employees are employed to provide services to customers, clients, patients, pupils or whoever else may be at the receiving end of what the institution has on offer, and within this obligation services can be provided with generosity of spirit as well as cost-effectively; the provision of services can be supplemented with love. And even the more abstract obligation to improve the efficiency and the cost-effectiveness of an institution can be supplemented by a concern to improve the ethos of the institution so that all the staff who work there and all the other people with whom the institution is in contact can have their scope for self-fulfilment enhanced.

However if these two kinds of opportunity were the sum total of the scope for reflecting God's love within the workplace, it would not be enough. There is a third kind of opportunity, less obvious but more important, which results from people's capacity for doing more than one thing at a time. There used to be a particular brand of toothpaste which, it was alleged, continued to benefit a person's teeth well after his brushing of them had stopped. The advertisements for the brand of toothpaste used to have pictures of people doing everyday things over captions like, "He is driving a bus and cleaning his teeth", and "She is typing a letter and cleaning her teeth". It is perfectly possible for a person to drive a bus or type a letter at the same time as loving and worshipping God; how this can happen is explained later.

People are people wherever they are and whether or not they may happen to be adopting an institutional role at the time, and friendship is friendship wherever it may blossom. A shared commitment to the furtherance of institutional objectives is capable of creating a special bond between people, which is the more valuable because it can unite people from very different backgrounds and who hold very different assumptions. The fact that a particularly intimate conversation may need to be broken off because the tea-break ends or because an institutional emergency arises may be an advantage rather than a drawback, because one thing that is more likely in paid employment than in most other environments is that the same people will be back together again tomorrow; a feature of work-based relationships is their capacity for being interrupted.

Differences in assumptions may make relating difficult in the first instance, but if relating can be achieved the differences become the source of enormous benefits. The shared workplace environment and values provide a sufficiently secure basis for the differences to be accommodated, and this provides an invaluable opportunity for mutual learning and consequent scope for an increased awareness of the variety of human condition, the breadth of God's creativity, and the need for personal humility. The reasons why people arrive in a particular workplace are to do with their competence in the performance of particular tasks, and so long as they are and remain competent there is no locus for sanctioned disapproval of whatever they may do outside working hours by way of antisocial behaviour or eccentric commitment; people of all religions and none, political extremists of right and left, adulterors and mysogynists, motorbike macchos and limp vegetarians, all are reduced to their common factor of task-based competence by the demands of the institution that employs them. What this offers the employed Christian is both the opportunity for getting to know a wide range of different sorts of people, and also the need to appreciate that moral disapproval is one of the least useful weapons in his armoury. He also cannot fail to appreciate that in his Christian commitment he is a member of a very small minority and that the non-Christian majority include some very fine people.

The committed Christian does, however, have one special contribution to make to the personal relationships he is able to form within the workplace. An awareness of God's love is a pervasive influence, and is likely to be visible to third parties and thus to affect the nature of relationships irrespective of whether this influence is overtly attributed. One of the effects of this awareness is that it gives a person a knowledge that he is loved and valued for his own sake irrespective of any valuation that he may drive from his competence in the performance of his institutional tasks, and irrespective of any role or status that the institution may confer upon him. There are many people whose sense of their own worth as human beings is so underdeveloped that they need to seek ways of boosting their self-valuation. This boosting may be achieved by a whole variety of devious means such as publicity seeking, sexual adventuring and even criminality, but employing institutions offer a particularly rich source of opportunities. Institutions offer role, status, power and the scope for competence in performance, and the importance of all of these is capable of being exaggerated so that they become a source of enhanced self-valuation. These are all high risk devices in that they take no account of the possibility of failure or the decline in capability that inevitably accompanies ageing, and in that they often give people a vested interest in the perpetuation of institutional practices with which they are familiar. Nevertheless these devices have the advantages of being publicly acceptable and even respected, and they probably carry a lower risk than some of the alternatives listed earlier; this means that they are commonly resorted to. A person whose reltionship with God is such as to obviate the need for resort to this kind of institutional dependance will have a great deal to offer people who are so dependant; this independence may often appear very threatening, but a person who knows about God's love will probably be capable of devising ways of developing relationships in which the threat is reduced.

All this is the background for a particular method of reflecting God's love in the workplace which is through pastoral care. Work absorbs a very high proportion of people's time and energy and is an important outlet for their creativity, and it is not surprising that when things go wrong, as they inevitably sometimes do, people should get very upset. The strong tradition of seeing work as a mechanistic activity means that very often such upsets take people completely by surprise, and help from someone within the workplace may be particularly welcome especially since a work-based pastor will be familiar with the culture of the workplace environment which is usually an essential aspect of the context within which the upset occurs. The things that go wrong may be directly related to the work itself, such as when a person is passed over for promotion or is given an incompatible assignment or makes a particular error of judgement, but they may also result from work-based personal relationships, for example when two colleagues are compelled by the requirements of the institution to work closely together and find that they cannot do so without getting severely on each other's nerves.

And also there are inevitably a number of people within any workplace who have so little in the way of a home base that they look to their employing institution for their primary personal relationships. They are likely to be at risk of overloading the relationships they are able to form at work; they will be looking for something of primary importance and are likely to be disappointed because most of the people they meet will have spouses, children or neighbours they are anxious to hurry off home to. A person who is aware of God's love will probably be able to take all this into account, since his relationship with God will enable him to take an objective view both of the people who are hungry for work-based relationships and of those who reject their overtures, and he will be able to understand and sympathise with both sets of needs. Nevertheless a discussion of the scipe for the exercise of pastorla care within the workplace needs to be prefaced by a number of caveats.

The first is that a person's primary relationship with his workplace colleagues is as colleague and not as pastor. This means that he must appreciate that he has no locus for being accepted as a pastor except on the basis of such personal respect that he has earned during the course of the relationship he has developed. It also means that it will be very unusual for pastoral care to be offered in anything resembling a formal setting; his colleagues are likely to be anxious to retain the semblance of the equality that is conferred by institutional relationships, and requests for help are less likely to be made in so many words as in suggestions to meet over lunch or in offers to buy a drink in a pub after work.

The second is that the care offered is often likely to be "off-site" in the sense that, if what people bring is a home-based problem, there will be no way in which a pastor will be able to see its home-based side; he will have to talk about marital problems without ever meeting the absent spouse, he will have to talk about errant teenage children without ever seeing either them or the local culture with which they may have identified, and he will have to talk about dependent senile relatives without ever being able to make his own assessment of their actual condition. All pastoral care requires an ability to distill a degree of objectivity from an inevitably subjective account, but nowhere is this ability more needed than in the workplace, particularly since the reason why a person deliberately seeks out a damp shoulder in the workplace may be because he is under the illusion that he will be able to present his own biased view of the problem without fear of contradiction.

The third is that different people inevitably view their workplace in different ways at different times, and a pastor needs to be sensitive to these variations. This difficulty may best be illustrated by four possible predicaments in which an employee who had just been widowed might find herself. One might be that she is weighted down at home by the need to appear rock-solid in relation to other members of her family, in which case work might be the only place where she can afford to break down in tears; the pastor would need to ensure that he does not necessarily perceive her as being on the verge of total collapse. Another might be that she is pressured at home into adopting a posture of exaggerated solemnity, in which case work might be the only place where she is able to balance this by talking about the ludicrous or ridiculous aspects of mourning; the pastor would have to ensure that he does not necessarily perceive her as frivolous. A third might be that at home she feels able to refer only to her husband's virtures, in which case work might be were she needs to vent her resentment and her anger; the pastor would need to ensure that he does not necessarily define the marriage as an unhappy one. And finally she might need to return to her workplace as a haven from the pressures of family bereavement, in which case she will welcome the opportunity to talk about something completely different or even to be left completely alone; the pastor would need to ensure that he does not necessarily perceive her as uncaring, and in particular he would need to ensure that he avoids the temptation to impose upon her his own need to be a pastor. All forms of pastoral care require sensitivity, and in the workplace particularly so since work is often an appropriately seen as an opportunity for balancing the demands of home.

And the fourth and most important caveat, already hinted at, is that there are a large number of people, both Christians and non-Christians, who would like to set themselves up as pastoral carers in order to meet their own need to feel helpful and valued, or because they are seeking an opportunity to project their own values onto other people. The damage such people are capable of perpetrating is very great. Very few would-be pastors in the workplace have had the benefit of any professional training in counselling since by definition they have chosen to work professionally at something else, so the importance of humility and self-awareness cannot be overstressed. It is important that pastoral care should develop naturally from personal relationships, and in particular it is important to counsel patience; luckily patience is comparatively easy to practice in the workplace because the person requiring help will almost certainly be back at work again tomorrow and because in the workplace there is always scope for diversion in that it is always possible to get on with the work.

For the most part, work-based pastoral care is likely to be responsive rather than initiatory, but there may be instances where deliberate intervention is called for. One obvious example is where a person may be behaving criminally or in breach of the institution's ethical code, and another, which is worth mentioning because it seems to be such a frequent phenomenon, is where there is work-based promiscuity. It is very easy for work-based relationships to become sexual because working together is capable of providing the basis for surprisingly deep attachments, and also because for many people there is an exaggerated demarcation between home and work which is capable of creating the illusion that home-based relationships and work-based relationships can be kept separate. This sort of promiscuity can be very damaging; work-based relationships are capable of developing very rapidly and taking people by surprise to the detriment of marriage and family ties, and there is a real risk of such relationships being lopsided, for example where a married man is seeking a work-based relationship as a pleasant diversion but where his spinster colleague treats it as a relationship of primary importance. There is also the problem of work-based promiscuity affecting work performance, both while the relationship is developing and more often while it is in the course of being broken off. Promiscuity is usually very easy for a pastor to identify, chiefly because so often so little effort is made to conceal it. Sometimes his help may be specifically requested, but sometimes he may feel that he needs to engineer an invitation to intervene. This will be a matter for his judgement, but where he decides that intervention is called for, an invitation will not usually be hard to come by. He needs however to ensure that in intervening he is not projecting his own moral values, particularly where what he may take for promiscuity is in fact a stable and valuable common-law relationship; the moral values of a Christian in this area are at risk of being somewhat austere.

A second particular method of reflecting God's love in the workplace is evangelism. A person who has discovered and appreciates God's love will feel an obligation to share this good news with other people, including with workplace colleagues. This obligation needs to be treated with a great deal of caution, chiefly because a Christian who is in contact with a cross-section of the population rather than with the unrepresentative samples found in church congregations needs to appreciate that for the majority of people any gratuitous mention of God is a turn-off. Nevertheless, the good news is there to be shared and it is news that is worth sharing.

A discussion of the scope for evangelism in the workplace needs, once again, to be prefaced by a number of caveats, and the first is the need to take proper account of the strong tradition of seeing Christianity as being to do with people in their homes and in their home communities and of seeing workplaces as the reserved dominion of Mammon. Within this tradition, the introduction of Christianity as a topic of conversation is seen as being at best irrelevant and at worst an affront in very bad taste.

The second is that, with a number of obvious exceptions such as denominational schools and religious bookshops, institutions are likely to mirror society at large which will mean that only a minute proportion of their staff will have been to a Christian church the previous Sunday and that only a barely larger proportion will ever have experienced any commitment to Christian worship. This means that the receptivity of most people is likely to be grounded in indifference and in some instances in extreme hostility; there are people around today whose churchgoing parents or grandparents didn't just drift away from Christianity but were driven out by ecclesiastical censoriousness. A church congregation that sees itself as being in some sense the elect has a tendency to define other people as being in some sense non-elect. These churches do not have to bother themselves very much with the people who have been cast out because by definition they aren't there, but they and their descendants are present in a variety of workplaces and this means that workplace evangelism often has to start somewhere the wrong side of square one.

The third caveat is that the primary relationship between a would-be evangelist and his workmates is and has to be that of colleagues. There are a great many employees who need to display some sort of idiosyncracy in the workplace in order to reinforce a need they may have to demonstrate that they are individuals in their own right and not merely cogs in the institutional machine; they may be overt in their support for a particular political viewpoint or a particular football club, or they may be ostentatious in their pursuit of jogging, philanthropy or darts. These idiosyncracies are usually tolerated with smiled indifference, which reflects the need felt by all workplace colleagues to get on with one another as comfortably as possible for as high a proportion as possible of the time they are together. There is a real risk that overt Christianity will be treated similarly to a harmless addiction to Queens Park Rangers. A Christian employee has to appreciate that his religious beliefs have no locus in the workplace, since he is in the workplace in order to work and not for any other reason.

And the fourth caveat is that people who have very little knowledge of Christianity are likely to have very warped ideas of what Christianity means, and to be so preoccupied with minutiae that they miss by miles any beginnings of an appreciation of the glorious unity of divine love. Warped ideas include the view that in order to believe in God it is necessary to eschew swearing, be teetotal, disapprove of heart transplants, or disobey strike calls, and that there is no longer any need for religion in the aftermath of Darwin, Freud, the holocaust, the welfare state, and the development of psychotherapy. Minutiae that loom large include the virgin birth, walking on water, birth control and abortion, investment in South Africa, WCC aid to freedom fighters, ownership of Soho brothels, and the philistinism of abandoning the Book of Common Prayer. And it is amazing how much agnostic interest in the mechanics of Christian belief has been generated by the Bishop of Durham.

The first two principles that underpin work-based evangelism have already been mentioned. The first is that evangelism has to take place within the context of the primacy of commitment to institutional objectives and values, and even taking into account what was said in Chapter 6 about the relationship between Christianity and institutional reform, a would-be evangelist must never forget that both he and his colleagues are paid to be in the workplace and paid to get the work done. And the second is that work-based evangelism, like work-based pastoral care, can only be effective if it is firmly rooted in relationships that have developed in a way that leads to the would-be evangelist being respected both as a colleague and as a person; the right to influence other people has to be earned, however good the news may be.

The third principle is that, in order to be effective, evangelism has to take place at a level where the two people involved are able to share common assumptions. If a would-be evangelist starts sounding off about the composition of the Trinity, the doctrine of damnation or the obligations of church attendance to somebody who cannot see the point of any of these, he is likely to written off as an over-enthusiastic faddist who is committed to something as irrelevant as fibre-based diets; marginally helpful no doubt but some way off being the panacea its adherents claim. Given the statistical probability that a large majority of workplace colleagues will never have gone regularly to Church, that some will be members of non-Christian religions and that only a few will ever have experienced any sort of Christian commitment, a great deal of tact and humility is required. Even the committed Christian minority is likely to be divided between those who are a genuine source of inspiration and support and those who see Christianity, however relevant it may be back at home, as having no place at work, and perhaps there will also be a few eccentrics whose attitudes and behaviour are an embarassment to everybody. There is scope for evangelism towards other Christians particularly where the aim is to demonstrate the presence of God in the workplace, but there is always the risk of the particularly bitter experience of being rejected by people who might have been expected to be allies. Relationships with members of other religions need to be initiated by a search for common ground, followed by an examination of differences that is undertaken in an ambience of mutual interest and respect.

Remarks about evangelism in relation to the statistical majority need to be prefaced by an exposition of the concept of pre-evangelism. The science of -isms prefixed by pre- has been developed most convincingly in nursery schools; children aged three and four are not yet ready to cope with being taught formal skills like reading, writing and mathematics, which would serve only to confuse them and cause them to miss out on more fundamental learning. They are therefore presented with opportunities for pre-reading, pre-writing and pre-mathematics. Reading requires being able to differentiate between the different shapes of the various letters, so pre-reading offers children shapes like squares, circles and triangles to differentiate between. Writing requires a degree of manual dexterity, so pre-writing encourages them in refining their drawing. Mathematics requires an understanding of concepts like division and subtraction and relative sizes, so in pre-mathematics the children are asked to make an equal pile of smarties for each child in the group and then take one away from each for the next time, and to try pouring water from the jug into the bottle, which will fit, and the water from the bottle into the jug, which will overflow. The points are first that these activities are at the level that the children have reached, and second that they are a useful preparation for the next stage. To go prematurely into the next stage, while it might make sense to ambitious parents and even to inexperienced teachers, would result in the children failing to appreciate what the next stage was properly about.

Pre-evangelism is designed for people who are not yet ready for evangelism. It needs to take place at the level that people have reached, and to be useful as preparation for the next stage which is evangelism proper. People who would reject the idea of the sinfulness of man can be helped to see that nobody is perfect. People who would reject the idea of repentance can be helped to see that it is better to be honest about shortcomings than to pretend they don't exist. People who would reject the idea of grace can be helped to see that human beings are capable of coping with demands and rising to occasions to a degree that no one would have thought possible. And people who would reject the idea of God can be encouraged to marvel and to wonder at the many things that are capable of being marvelled and wondered at. Pre-evangelism concentrates on the ingredients of Christian belief without resort to Christian jargon. The practice of it is likely to benefit not only those on the receiving end of it but also to those who expound it, since the challenge of having to express familiar truths in unfamiliar language will inevitably be a valuable experience.

And the fourth principle is the importance of mutual honesty and mutual respect. Workplace relationships are for the most part grounded in a high degree of personal contact and in a high degree of mutual awareness of each other's competence in the performance of institutional tasks; this is capable of providing a basis for mutual honesty about attitudes towards the tasks that are required and about competence levels. This in turn can permit the extension of the relationship to include a comparably honest approach towards personal reactions to a broader range of experiences both within and outside the institution, which in turn can lead to discussion and examination of the frameworks within which these reactions and attitudes are related and made sense of. People who are capable of holding down a job are usually capable of creating for themselves such a framework, and the effort that has gone in to this needs to be respected. There is no place for an evangelistic attitude that implies that my framework is better than yours; what is necessary is an interest in other people's frameworks, initially for their own sakes, and perhaps later in order to provide a basis for a comparison with Christian belief. In this context, an exposition of Christian belief is likely to be accepted and respected, including where this requires an admission of difficulty or doubt.

When these four principles are respected, it is remarkable how effective work-based evangelism can be. The common core of shared work-based experience provides an invaluable foundation for the building of personal relationships, and these are important because of the likelihood that interest will be concentrated more on the Christian than on Christianity. A would-be evangelist is obliged to demonstrate an awareness of the love of God as being something that has affected him for the better.

The second kind of opportunity for reflecting God's love in the workplace is by means of supplementing the performance of institutional tasks, so that the performance of such tasks becomes enhanced by the addition of love. It must, however, be recognised once again that in institutional terms the competent performance of the required tasks is paramount, and this means that love has to be in addition to competent performance and is in no sense a substitute for it. There are two main areas of work where this sort of scope exists; one is the addition of love to management, and the other is the addition of love to the provision of services to customers, clients, patients, pupils, or whoever.

The Christian manager's primary obligation in the workplace, like that of any other manager, is to manage, and to ensure that the staff he is responsible for perform their required tasks competently so that the institution's objectives are met. His managerial task will be in part impersonal and in part personal. The impersonal part comes first, and it requires the assessment of those institutional objectives for which he is responsible and the translation of them into performable tasks which, if successfully performed, will result in the objectives being met. He then has to translate these performable tasks into the work which his staff will actually have to do. The personal part involves also allocating this work between the staff who are already employed and taking action as necessary to correct any mismatch, for example by arranging the transfer or dismissal of existing staff, recruiting new staff, and arranging training. He then has to see that the people to whom the work has eventually been allocated actually do it. The impersonal and the personal bits have to be this way round, because otherwise there would be a risk of the subjective view of work taking primacy over the objective view; the effect of this might be that tasks were defined and allocated on the basis of what the existing staff most enjoyed rather than on the basis of how the institution's needs might best be met. Nevertheless, both the allocation of tasks and the business of ensuring that they are competently performed require that the staff concerned be seen as people as well as cogs in the institutional machine, and a personal relationship between a manager and the staff who work to him is an important element in the achievement of institutional objectives. From the institution's point of view, the purpose of the personal relationships is to enable the tasks to be performed effectively, but even though this purpose is limited it must not be thought that personal relationships are totally outside the institution's concern. Even when viewed from an institutional standpoint, good management includes quite a bit of what often passes for loving. It includes fairness and openness, and, to borrow a Pauline phrase, it includes long-temperedness. It also includes encouraging staff to give of their best and taking seriously difficulties they may have, and this will include flexibility in the enforcing of requirements up to the point, which must not be transgressed in any event, where institutional objectives are jeopardised. All of these imply some knowledge of each employee as an individual person, since the nature of the constraints on good performance will be different in each individual case. And also, bearing in mind that the expression of love by definition requires that the lover put himself out for the beloved, a loving manager must remember not to put himself out to the extent of neglecting any aspect of his own institutional performance.

Having said all of this, there is still scope for the expression of love in management. Love involves seeing a person as a whole person and not just as an institutional performer. This adds a further dimension to relationships and offers scope, albeit within the constraints already mentioned, for combining management with pastoral care which goes beyond a concern for improving institutional performance. But the most important expression of love in management is a loving manager's capacity for identifying with his staff's predicaments, for feeling the pain where demands, institutional and otherwise, grate upon individuality, and for feeling joy where limitations are overcome and performance, institutional and otherwise, is raised. This empathy is particularly important where a manager is required to discipline a member of staff, and particularly where he is required to sack him. Once a decision has been made to sack someone the institution has no further interest in him, and though a loving manager has no alternative but to proceed with dismissal where dismissal is required, his empathy will dictate that his concern continues. Empathy is a highly visible expression of love and is likely to be both helpful and appreciated, and it is very demanding. It is particularly valuable where it takes the form of giving a dismissed employee the opportunity to vent his anger; one of the most personally damaging consequences of a summary dismissal is that no opportunity is given to the person who is dismissed to be angry with the institution that has dismissed him, which means that unless a loving manager is willing to put himself in the firing line the anger is likely to be directed inappropriately towards the ex-employee's family and friends.

The other way in which institutional requirements may be supplemented by love is in the provision of services, and the scope for this is most obvious in the caring professions. Once again, it must be said that the competent performance of institutional tasks does require that an interest be taken in clients as people; doctors and nurses are required to treat and care for the whole patient, teachers are required to educate the whole child, and social workers are required to concern themselves with the whole client. This concern in each case extends also to families and friends. Outside the caring professions, shop assistants and bus conductors and anybody else who has direct contact with clients is required to be polite at all times and to take an interest in clients' predicaments where in the longer term this would benefit the institution. Not to do this would not just be unloving, it would also be unprofessional and in breach of contractual obligations.

The constraints on loving in the context of the provision of services are the same as those on loving in the context of management in that primacy has to be given to institutional needs. A district nurse may go out of her way to meet a patient's personal needs as well as nursing him, but her contract requires her not to spend a long time with one patient at the expense of the next. A DHSS desk clerk may take an interest in a client's personal predicament as well as assessing him for benefit, but he mustn't forget about the other clients in the queue. A municipal gardener may see the District Council's park as an opportunity for a horticultural celebration of God's love for his created world, but he has to sweep the playground as well as manuring the dahlias if that is what the Council requires him to do. And as well as allocating their time in accordance with their terms and conditions of service, all three are obliged to maintain the dignity, the impartiality and the integrity of their various callings; the district nurse has to carry out and record the required nursing procedures as well as anything else helpful she may choose to do, the desk clerk must not assess the client as being eligible for more money than the criteria allow however great his sympathy may be for the client's financial needs, and the gardener has to plant the dahlias in a way that will ensure that they actually grow. When a doctor is required to concern himself with the whole patient, this is on the assumption that the whole patient is relevant to the treatment of his disease, and when a teacher is required to be concerned with the whole child, this is on the assumption that the whole child is relevant to his education; this degree of professional concern is an institutional requirement which has to be gone through in any event, but the supplementing of this with love permits a broader concern. Once again, it is the empathy that matters. A patient will feel loved if he is able to perceive in the eyes of the doctor whom he has trusted with his care a concern which extends to a sharing in his pain, not just in the pain that is the symptom of his illness, but perhaps also that deeper pain which is the manifestation of having been let down by a body which, however frail, is the only vehicle he has which is capable of conveying him on his journey through the world.

A further point that needs to be made is that both managers and front-line staff are institutionally required to concern themselves only with those people for whom they are managerially or professionally responsible. A manager who is aware of an employee in difficulty who is not below him in line management but is answerable to somebody else will have no managerial locus for intervention, and a district nurse will have no professional locus for looking after a patient on another district nurse's list, however great his need. It is possible that there may be scope for offering a little covert interstitial help in such circumstances, but there is likely to be an institutional requirement that has to be accorded primacy which forbids the crossing of demarcation lines.

The development of loving relationships in the workplace and the supplementing with love of institutional tasks are indubitably important, but if, as was said at the beginning of this chapter, these represented the entire scope for the reflection of God's love in the workplace, this would not be enough. This is because these two forms of loving are essentially peripheral to the performance of institutional tasks and are not an integral part of them. The performance of institutional tasks takes up too high a proportion of people's energy and time to be removed entirely from man's response to God. The third kind of opportunity for the reflection of God's love in the workplace makes use of people's capacity for doing more than one thing at a time, and there are two things that can be done simultaneously with work. One is worshipping and the other is loving, and both are the expression of an attitude rater than the performing of additional activities. The Christian word for them is intercession, and intercession has a central relevance to being a Christian in paid employment.

Intercession occurs at many levels, but unfortunately many Christians have not got beyond seeing it in terms of the formal prayers of the sort that happen between the creed and the peace in the Holy Communion Rite A of the ASB, prayers that take the form of asking God to do the sort of things one would normally have expected him to be doing anyway. I was initiated into intercession's deeper meaning during a panted conversation in the middle of a half-marathon, when I found myself running alongside a man wearing a vest inscribed "Jogging for Jesus". I summoned sufficient breath to tell him I was a clergyman and to ask him what the inscription meant, and he explained that as he saw it the post-resurrection Jesus was incapable of experiencing human activities such as half-marathon running except insofar as human beings experienced them on his behalf. He then overtook me and I never saw him again, which was a pity as I would have liked to have explored further with him this theology of long-distance running, but he gave me the insight I was looking for; intercession is experiencing as much as possible of what it means to be human and consciously offering it back to God.

Paid employment provides rich opportunities for intercessionary worship and for intercessionary loving. Work represents to an extent the realisation of human potential; for many people their paid employment is an important opportunity for putting themselves effectively into practice, and even people who don't enjoy what they are paid to do do at least do something. And practically all paid employment is a process of meeting needs, of cultivating the earth in such a way as to make life more fruitful for the people who live on it. Combining work with intercessionary worship means being aware of all this and feeling joy, not only when a colleagure overcomes a particular difficulty or does something particularly well, but also in response to the routine procedures through which people express themselves daily. Combining work with intercessionary worship means experiencing joy at the way in which useful things are produced and distributed and services are provided so that the earth continues to give of its goodness and so that the gift of life in all its richness goes on. And Christian worship in the workplace means identifying all this joy with the creator God who in his bounty no only made it all possible but enabled it all actually to happen.

Intercessionary worship is on balance a joyful experience, but intercessionary loving is on balance painful. The Christian tradition has long recognised that whatever its potential the world is far from perfect for the people who live in it, and that the imperfections lead not just to human suffering but to human damage. The suffering and the damage is partly the result of the natural world having no special respect for human needs; volcanoes explode, rivers flood, storms rage and the sun beats down irrespective of the fact that this may ruin people's lives. And partly they are caused by the deliberate destructiveness of individual people. But for the most part they are the result of the cumulative effect of decisions made in ignorance or in unconcern for their impact on others. Part of the worshipping aspect of work is the joy in the progress that man has made in limiting the destructive effects of the elements, but the elements are in no sense subject to human control and disasters continue to happen; part of intercessionary loving is identifying with the suffering that results. Part of the worshipping aspect of work is the joy in the progress that men have made in their capacity to live and work together, but evil still occurs; part of intercessionary loving is identifying with the suffering that results from this also. And for all the good things that have resulted from the cumulative output of institutions, it has to be recognised that a high proportion of the pain and the damage that people experience can be directly attributed to institutions' ignorance, unconcern and limited vision; the most significant aspect of intercessionary loving in the workplace is identifying with the suffering that results from this.

There is the suffering of an institution's employees, both the suffering that results from the unfairness and the inconsiderateness that are inherent within systems, and the suffering that results from hopes and creativity being thwarted either because there is no place for them within a particular institution or because a particular institution is too crass to tap them. Then there are the thwarted ambitions and aspirations of employees who, with or without justification, feel that they could rise higher, and there is the perversion that is perpetrated in certain institutions which impose too brutally their value systems upon staff who are not in a position to protect their own human instincts. And more specifically there is the suffering that happens when the institution's values clash with an employee's deeply held convictions. It was suggested earlier that the proper course for an employee who could not reconcile his personal beliefs with his institutional obligations would be to resign and seek alternative employment, but while this view may make sense in theory it is not always that simple in practice; alternative employment may not be easy to find, so resignation may mean an unsupported family with all the damage this is capable of causing, and resignation may mean leaving other colleagues behind to cope unaided in a destructive situation. Dag Hammerskjold once compared resignation on a matter of principle with Jesus coming down from the cross; there are instances where adherence to principles is the easier option and where staying on, perhaps with strengthened determination to strive for reform, is the braver and more admirable course however great the pain may be.

And there is the suffering by the clients of institutions, clients who are damaged by institutional failings like hospital patients who are wrongly diagnosed or treated by their doctors, like schoolchildren who fail to get a university place because they have been inadequately taught in the sixth form, like prisoners who become recidivists on discharge because of the inhumanity of their prison experience, and like cheated shoppers who are unable to get recompense because of carefully drafted small print. And there are clients whose needs the institution cannot meet because there are insufficient resources available for it to be able to do its job as well as it could, like renal patients who die because of a shortage of haemodialysis facilities, like schoolchildren who cannot be taught science because there is not enough money to equip laboratories, like prisoners whose self-esteem is destroyed because of inhumane prison conditions, and shoppers whose wants are not in stock. And then there are the clients whose needs are beyond the scope of any institution however effective like patients whose illnesses are terminal especially if they are ill-equipped to face the prospect of death, like schoolchildren who because of genetic disabilities or damaging home backgrounds are ineducable, like prisoners who are delinquent both outside and inside prison, and like shoppers who do not have the money to buy what they really need.

And finally there is the more general suffering that happens within an institution's purview, whether caused by institutional omission, like the wars and famines that might have been prevented by more effective international agencies, or by commission, like the poverty which is created by the pursuit of inflationary policies or the unemployment that is created by the pursuit of deflationary ones. And many institutions operate on such a large scale that even when they work successfully for the general good there are a certain number of people who are unfortunate enough to get in the way and who suffer merely because they don't fit in with the institutional overview of things, like people whose homes happen to be in the path of a projected motorway.

So there are many sorts of suffering that can be witnessed from within institutions, suffering that is caused by callousness or inefficiency, suffering that might be prevented if the institution were adequately resourced or could work magic, and suffering that happens on the dark side of doing the right thing. Individual people who work within institutions are aware of a greater or lesser amount of this suffering. In a few instances they may be able to do something practical to alleviate it, either by doing their job a little bit better, or by supplementing their work with a little bit of added love, but more often than not it seems that there is nothing they can do except accept it or pretend that it isn't there. However the point about God's love is that there is something practical that can be done in such circumstances, because intercession is something real and tangible. A person who is aware of God's love for his created world and for the people who inhabit it will appreciate that this love is irrespective of the scope for remedial action. A closer identification with God will lead to a closer identification with people, and to a sharing in their joys and in particular in their suffering. An identification with this suffering will lead to remedial action where this is appropriate and possible, but will continue even when there is no scope for such action. It is an identification that is wearing and imposes heavy burdens, but access to God's inexhaustible resources enables this burden to be borne.

In some instances, this identification may have beneficial results, even if they are not the remedial results that were initially looked for. There is a difference for a terminally ill patient being told his prognosis by a doctor who identifies with his predicament and thus makes his concern plain, and being told by one who chooses to protect himself by distancing himself and treating the telling as a purely mechanical task. And a child who does not have enough money for what he wants to buy would prefer having this pointed out by a shopkeeper who appreciated the tragedy rather than by one who saw him solely as a time-wasting nuisance. And there are occasions when the only beneficiaries of the identification are the employee's colleagues; I still remember with intense gratitude the tears of the Executive Officer described on this book's opening page.

But there will still be a large number of occasions when identification with suffering can have no apparent practical benefits whatever, and even in these circumstances the identification is still worthwhile and is still a positive action in its own right. The beneficiaries are God and the intercessor. Chapter 2 suggested that pain is felt by God whenever his will is denied and people suffer, and he cannot but be helped when other people share this pain by means of intercession. And the intercession is beneficial to the intercessor, who is rendered more truly human both through the realisation of his capacity for identifying with the common lot of humanity and through his closer identification with God.

Chapter 2 also showed how paid employment gives people the opportunity, through their work, for becoming more fully human and thus for worshipping God and coming closer to him, but Chapter 5 made the further point that working within the constraints of a contract of employment provides very little opportunity for the expression of love. This chapter has attempted to extend the framework for integrating paid employment and Christian belief by showing that there is in fact scope for the expression of love in paid employment in two minor ways, through the development of personal relationships and through the supplementing of work activity, and in one way that is major, fundamental and pervasive, through identification with the people who are in contact with institutions and through empathy with the effects that the institutions have on them. Many people find themselves experiencing this identification, and both the joy and the pain of it, without necessarily meaning to; this is admirable and helpful, but the necessary further step is the conscious offering of this experience back to God in intercession. This particular sort of intercession is the special contribution of institutionally employed Christians since Christians who are not in institutional employment will have difficulty in understanding the nature of institutions and their impact on people, and will be less able to manage the identification effectively. Without an appreciation of the nature and the importance of intercession it is difficult to find within paid employment sufficient Christian meaning and sufficient Christian purpose to sustain the high proportion of our total time and effort which we spend at work.

8

Integration Two:
Ordained Ministry in the Workplace

An increasing proportion of the men and women who train for the ordained ministry do so during their spare time while continuing in secular paid employment, and an increasing proportion of ordained clergy are exercising their ministry while in secular rather than in Church employ. These trends seem set to continue, and it is important that their implications be worked out sooner rather than later because there are a number of problems inherent in how these people view the exercise of their ministry and in how it is viewed by the Church as a whole. I am aware that the language and the illustrations used in this chapter are essentially Anglican; I apologise for the narrowness of this perspective and hope that readers from other denominations can make the necessary adjustments and still find echoes of their experience. And I am aware that I tend to talk about priesthood which in the Anglican Church at this moment in time excludes the ministry of all women and of those men who have opted for the distinctive diaconate; my apologies for this are less profuse since, while I admire the honesty of those who have chosen to be excluded from the priesthood and grieve with those who are excluded from it against their choice, priesthood is a crucial component of ordained ministry and for many people is what ordained ministry is primarily about.

There are essentially four models of ordained ministry. The first is the parochial ministry where clergy receive a stipend from the Church to enable them to minister to the people who live within a defined geographical area. Even though most of the people who live in a particular parish are unlikely ever to have had any contact with the parish church, and even though the demarcation implied by parish boundaries has been eroded almost into meaninglessness by improvements in transport and by rural and inner-city depopulation, this remains the model that is in the forefront of people's minds whenever ordained ministry is spoken of, and it tends to provide the yardstick against which other models of ministry are judged. The parochial ministry is still fundamental to the functioning of the Church, but other models of ministry are in no way obliged to conform to its particular traditional patterns.

The second model is the specialist ministry where clergy are employed to exercise a ministry to specified groups of people on a basis that is not geographical. This includes clergy who are employed by particular institutions that are of the view that the presence of an ordained ministry will be of benefit to the institution concerned; there are hospital chaplains employed by health authorities, prison chaplains employed by the Prison Service, school and university chaplains employed by the schools and universities they serve, and chaplains to the armed services employed by the Ministry of Defence. It also includes clergy who are employed by a church or a church-related body to work with a particular group of people such as teenagers or the elderly or the homeless or drug addicts. And it also includes clergy who are employed in industrial missions. An important point about this model of ordained ministry is that priests are employed as priests to do priestly things even though they may do many other things as well which may not seem particularly priestly at first sight. This means that there is no essential conflict of role even though these clergy may experience a whole variety of difficulties in making their priestly ministry effective.

The third model is the auxiliary parochial ministry where clergy continue in secular employment and receive no income from the Church but see their ordained ministry as a spare-time one within the parochial structure. At first glance this model would seem to avoid conflicts of role, but there is an intrinsic difficulty in that it assumes that time spent in paid employment is somehow irrelevant to the exercise of ordained ministry. This book makes the alternative assumption that there is plenty of scope for the exercise of ordained ministry in the course of paid employment, and the implication of this is that there would in fact be a serious conflict of role if a priest were to go off to work without attempting to exercise a priestly ministry while he was there.

And the fourth model is the non-stipendiary ministry, or the ministry of priest-workers as they are nowadays sometimes called, who continue in secular employment, usually with a parochial link, but who see their workplace as being a particular focus for their ministry of at least comparable importance to their parish, and it is with this fourth model that this chapter is concerned. A priest-worker will have been employed to perform purely secular tasks, and the exercise of his priestly ministry will have to happen within the context of the primacy of his contractual obligations; from the point of view of his employing institution the fact that he is ordained will be at best irrelevant and at worst a potential source of complication. This means that the institution has the right to expect from an employed priest not only that he give priority to the competent performance of his institutional tasks, but also that he work within the required institutional value system and that he adopt as appropriate the required institutional role; these expectations inevitably constrain the exercise of priestly ministry and inevitably lead to tension.

The requirement that priority be given to the competent performance of institutional tasks is significant chiefly in that getting the job done takes up time. One aspect of ministry that is capable of absorbing a great deal of a priest-worker's time is his ministry to individuals which, of course, has to be compressed within the constraints imposed by workplace demands. A distraught colleague once came to see me in the middle of a morning to say that his son had just been arrested on a drugs charge; I was working on something important at the time which had to be submitted by lunch-time, but I put up a holding reply and heard him out. I got away with it in the sense that I wasn't criticised for having missed the deadline, but in retrospect it would have been much better if I had made it clear that both my colleague and I were employed to get the work done and if I had postponed the conversation till the lunch-break; the man was feeling that he was a lousy father and it would probably have helped him if he could at least have felt that he was a responsible civil servant. Another aspect of ministry that takes up time is concern for workplace ethos, and a priest-worker who decides to concentrate his energies on this would perhaps be well advised to to seek a position within personnel management or a trade union office since either of these would ensure that he had both the time and the locus for making his influence felt.

The requirement that all employees work within the institution's value system presents greater difficulties since conflicts between this and the values implied by God's love are inevitable. A distinction needs to be drawn between those workplace values that are contrary to the institution's ethics and those which are inherent in the institution's purpose. A priest-worker has every obligation to oppose practices however widespread that involve fiddling expense accounts or short-changing customers, but these obligations are shared by all employees. On the other hand he has to accept and live with assumptions such as the desirability of a washing machine in every home, and if he finds such assumptions intolerable he should resign. If, as is more likely, he finds them acceptable but somewhat short of the whole truth, he should not seek to undermine them since this would jeopardise the institution's purpose, and he should find some way of coping with the tensions. A proper reaction to the limitations inherent in many institutional assumptions will be to feel sad about them and perhaps to share this sadness with one or two trusted colleagues, but the most useful course of action will be to seek to understand the full implications of such limitations, to identify with the human suffering that they cause, and to offer this up to God in intercession. The same will be true in relation to all the shortcomings of the institution whether they be due to the institution's inherent inefficiency, or to the limited resources available to it, or to inadequacy resulting from the limitations of human knowledge and skill. But one cautionary note; not all apparent conflicts between institutional and Christian values are real. A priest-worker friend of mine who works for a building society has to assess applicants for mortgages against criteria handed down to him from head office. During his first few months in this particular job he experienced a great deal of pain whenever he had to say no to people who wanted mortgages, especially if they were newly married couples, because he could imagine so clearly what difficulties the rejection would cause. He coped with this pain by deriding head office and he condemned the criteria as un-Christian. Emboldened in his righteous anger, he then started to interpret the criteria more flexibly and, as he saw it, in a more Christian way. He then had the very disturbing experience of a young couple, to whom he had given a mortgage following a flexible interpretation of the criteria, defaulting on their payments and their house being repossessed; this got the couple into far greater difficulties than they would have been in if they had been refused a mortgage in the first place. This made my friend realise that the head office criteria were in fact quite sensible, that the interpretation of the criteria however flexibly was part of his institutional responsibility, and that the better he did his job the happier everybody would be.

And there is the requirement that all employees adopt an institutional role. The most overt symbol of an institutional role is a uniform. Soldiers, judges, policemen, nurses and the people who ring up shopping at a supermarket check-out all have a very clear institutional role and all wear uniform; it would cause a lot of difficulty if people who weren't employed in these particular institutional roles were to assume responsibility for these particular institutional tasks, so it is right that the tasks should be performed only by people who are wearing the appropriate uniform. The uniform of the priesthood is the dog-collar; when anybody sees a dog-collar they immediately say "priest" and their conditioned reactions are triggered. The role of the civil servant is to represent the interests of the Government of the day, but if a priest-civil servant were to wear a dog-collar during working hours this would inevitably suggest a different role, that of representing the Church; to some people this might imply that he was fundamentally critical of Government policy, and to others it might imply that the Government was acting with Church approval, and in either case his role as a civil servant would be jeopardised. There is also the risk that wearing a dog-collar during institutional employment might compromise the Church; a personnel officer wearing a dog-collar while laying off staff might create the impression that the redundancy policy carried Church backing, and a salesman in a dog-collar might create the impression that his particular brand carried the seal of divine approval. Priest-workers need to appreciate that while they are about their institutional business it is their institutional business that matters and that this requires them to give primacy to their institutional role. And it is perfectly possible to exercise a priestly role without wearing a dog-collar to reinforce it.

Nevertheless, priest-workers will need to be known as priests to their workplace colleagues because being so known is an important aspect of their Christian witness, and without being so known the availability of what they have on offer would be severely restricted. And another reason is that a surprisingly large number of people seem to feel betrayed when they discover that somebody they had previously thought of as a colleague is in fact a priest as well. In the main the people who feel this seem to be at one or other extreme of the spectrum; there are those devout churchgoers who feel that a priest ought to be more special than someone they work alongside, and there are those non-churchgoers who have an atavistic fear of the priesthood as an army of professional disapprovers and who feel that a priest spying out their weaknesses in the workplace, which should be the ultimate sanctuary from such intrusion, is betrayal indeed. Perhaps the best solution to the dog-collar problem is a discrete lapel cross or chirho badge which is not so obvious as to define a person's primary role, but which is at least a sign for those who know what it means and a talking point for those who don't.

What a priest-worker has to live with in the workplace is his colleagues' preconceived images of the priesthood, whether they be grounded in adulation, hostility or indifference. Some of these images are father-figure projections, which mean that the priest-worker may find himself at the receiving end of efforts to impress or required to express the moral disapproval that a person is unable to express for himself; these projections, however disconcerting they may be initially for a priest-worker whose reactions are neither approving or disapproving, are nonetheless overt enough to be worked with and can form the basis for a helpful relationship. Sometimes the images are based on television portrayals by Brian Rix or Derek Nimmo, and the priest-worker is expected to be naive and other-worldly and to have trousers that are likely to fall down. But more often than not the images are based on an extension of the parochial priesthood, perhaps because the roles and functions of the parochial priesthood are reasonably clear and broadly accepted and this creates first a temptation to define priesthood in terms of the roles and functions of the parochial clergy, and then to apply this perception to priest-workers and to find them more or less wanting.

Nevertheless it is worth working through a list of these images since they provide an opportunity to examine the extent to which they are or aren't applicable to priest-workers. Perhaps the most popularly held image of a priest is as a person in charge of a church. Apart from a few priest-teachers who may be employed in schools that have chapels, this manifestly does not apply to priest-workers since altars are not a standard piece of workplace equipment. An extension of this image, and one which has a more ancient historical base, it that of a priest as the focial point of a worshipping congregation. Once again, this does not easily apply to priest-workers and there is in fact a strong case for specifically disapplying it, since it would imply that priest-workers were under some sort of obligation to gather round themselves a worshipping congregation of workplace colleagues to be the focal point of. A priest-worker who approached his employment with this objective in the forefront of his ministerial ambitions would be unlikely to be successful and would almost certainly run into conflict with his contractual obligations. Where a worshipping congregation does exist within a workplace in any permanent fashion, it is likely to have developed as the culmination of a series of individual relationships.

A second popular image of a priest is that of a person who cares for the people of his parish. For the priest-worker the equivalent of parishioners are his workplace colleagues, and the scope for pastoral care in the workplace was examined in the previous chapter. A pastoral ministry in the workplace will be different from a pastoral ministry in the parish, but nonetheless potentially valuable and rewarding. The main constraints will be the invasive primacy of contractual obligations and the inappopriateness in many instances of pastoral care being exercised as an overt act of Christian witness, and the main potential advantages will be the continuity and the catholicity of workplace relationships and the fact that care will stem from an equal relationship between colleagues. The benefits of such relationships are, of course, two-way since they enable people who would otherwise never meet a priest to have day-to-day contact with one, and since they enable the priest-worker to broaden his understanding of the range of possible human attitudes and predicaments and to make this experience available to the rest of the Church.

A third image, consequent upon the second, is that of a priest as an impressario who performs rite-of-passage ceremonies and the scope for priest-workers to conduct baptisms, marriages and funerals seem to be greater than might have been imagined. The beneficiaries of such sacraments seem to be in the main workplace colleagues who are on the fringes of church membership and who see sacramental rites of passage as being important, sometimes no doubt as a result of contact with the priest-worker concerned, but who are not sufficiently committed to a particular parish church to turn automatically to its priest. There are workplace colleagues who have babies, who get married and remarkably frequently who get married to each other, and who die; a bereaved family may well turn to a priest-worker who they knew knew him, perhaps to conduct the funeral service or more usually to assist either at the funeral or at a memorial service in order to represent the work-based aspect of his life. Events such as these present real opportunities for pastoral care and evangelism, and also for a priest-worker to demonstrate his priestliness not only to the families concerned but also to other workplace colleagues who are invited to participate. There is always, of course, the point of detail as to whether these ceremonies should happen in the church to which the priest-worker is attached or in the family's parish church; if the latter there will need to be liaison between the priest-worker and the parish priest.

A particular sacrament that needs to be mentioned in this context is the sacrament of confession. The tradition of individual sacramental confession exists within Roman Catholicism and as a minority tradition within the Church of England, but because of the probable range of his workplace contacts it is as well for a priest-worker who does not himself come from within this tradition to prepare himself for the hearing of confessions. There are quite a number of sins committed in the workplace, by people acting both on their own account and in the name of their employing institutions; their perpetrators, whether or not they come from a confessing tradition, are likely to see a priest-colleague as somebody in whom they can safely and therapeutically confide, particularly since he will be familiar with the institutional culture and background. There may also be people who wish to talk to a priest-colleague about home-based sins simply because of his separateness from them. Some people may come to the priest-worker with a wish to confess already formulated, but there may be others who wish initially merely to talk about a problem and the priest-worker may wish to suggest sacramental confession as a conclusion. It is absolutely crucial that roles be properly clarified, partly because the priest will need to effect a change from being a colleague to being a confessor, partly because of the need to effect a properly demarcated transition from an informal to a formal relationship, and partly also because of the very real risk that the perpetrator of a work-based sin may try to implicate the priest in what he has done by confiding in him under the seal of the confessional. The priest will need to ensure that the ground rules are clearly understood and agreed by both parties before he adopts the confessorial role, and in some instances may need to spell out the dilemma between his priestly and contractual obligations. It may be helpful for the priest to signal the moment of transition, for example by putting on his stole or even by going with his colleague for the formal part of the confession to a nearby church. Once the confessorial role has been adopted, the seal of the confessional is, of course, absolute, but where the sin confessed is a breach of institutional ethics or discipline, the priest would have the option of withholding absolution or making absolution conditional upon the breach being reported in accordance with institutional procedures.

A fourth popular image of a priest is that of an evangelist. The scope for work-based evangelism, and for pre-evangelism, was discussed in the previous chapter, but a point that is worth repeating is that the main advertisement for what the priest-worker has on offer is the priest-worker himself. This puts a high premium on how a priest-worker conducts himself, including on the manner in which he performs his contractual tasks. Since perfection both as a person and as a worker is unattainable, both for priest-workers and for everybody else, this requires that one of the most significant weapons in the priest-worker's armoury is honesty about his own shortcomings. However at the same time it is desirable that he earn the respect of his colleagues both as a person and as a worker, since so much of his concern will be with work-related matters that it will be necessary for him to demonstrate both a competence in and an understanding of institutional issues. This will make things a bit difficult for him if he is promoted or transferred to work that is new to him, but since promotion and transfer are likely to be common workplace phenomena it will be important that he experience the problems involved; there is no basis on which he should turn down such opportunities merely in order to safeguard a competent image; it would, though, be as important for him as for everybody else to take steps to avoid being promoted to a level beyond his competence. Many of his colleagues, non-churchgoers as well as churchgoers, will look to him as an example of personal and institutional morality, and the latter is as important as the former; institutional ethics, as has been said already, offer an opportunity for effective worship and are compatible with Christian morality even if they are not derived from Christian principles in a narrowly defined sense.

A further point about workplace evangelism is that workplace colleagues are very likely to look to a priest-worker for help on specifically spiritual matters; a priest-worker is seen by many as a lone bastion of spirituality in a world where spiritual values are not particularly in evidence, and this may serve both to awaken a need and to suggest a means of meeting it. Let two actual but over-simplified instances suffice as examples of what a priest-worker may be asked to provide. The first concerns a middle manager who was in the process of coming to terms with the fact that he had reached in his early forties the level beyond which he was most unlikely to be promoted further. Up to that point, in his institutional life at least, his primary purpose had been to get himself noticed as a high achiever and to win promotion, and his efforts in this respect had been rewarded. He then realised that further efforts would no longer be met with similar reward, so he started casting about for an alternative sense of purpose and sensed that Christianity was capable of filling this need. The second concerns a civil servant on the social security side of the DHSS who had started his working live with a vision of how the social security system, by providing certain guaranteed levels of income, might significantly reduce and then perhaps eliminate human suffering. As he worked his way up the institutional hierarchy to levels of increasing responsibility, he came to see that his personal contibution, though on balance helpful rather then unhelpful, did not increase proportionally in the way he had hoped; he was forced to realise that for the most part the misery that accompanies poverty is incapable of alleviation by means of social security. He then sought a framework which made sense of human suffering and which was not dependant upon his beneficent intervention, and he sensed that Christianity might provide it. In both these instances the people concerned became aware of the limitations of their institutions, in the first case in providing an individual sense of purpose and in the second in providing scope for meaningul activity, and they sought a more comprehensive framework. It was comparatively easy to give both of them intellectual explanations of how an awareness of God's love can provide the basis of such a framework, in the first case his love for the person concerned and in the second his love for people below the poverty line, and of how this love can be focussed in the Eucharist; both of them were then interested in trying the framework for themselves out to see if it worked.

And a final image of a priest is as the president at the Eucharist. The parish priest is well used to celebrating the Eucharist among and for his congregation, but this privilege is less obvious for the priest-worker. It may happen that a group of people emerges from the workplace who wish to gather for the Eucharist, and there is something special about such a celebration among colleagues in a canteen or a committee room, but as with other Christian groupings in the workplace it is important that the pace isn't forced. It is also possible that there may be a regular lunch-time or after-work Eucharist in a nearby church where the priest-worker is able to celebrate and which a number of his colleagues are able to attend. However for the most part a priest-worker's celebration of the Eucharist is likely to be in a setting that is not linked directly with his workplace concerns; he is likely to exercise his practical ministry with one set of people, his workplace colleagues, and his liturgical ministry with a completely different set of people, the congregation of his parish church. This creates tensions; I personally am always aware that the congregation has little share in what I bring from my workplace to the altar of my parish church. And it is a source of sadness, particularly bearing in mind the importance of the intercessionary aspects of workplace ministry. But nevertheless the Eucharist has a universal relevance and its meaning is not constrained by time or place, and wherever it is celebrated it is the essential process through which a priest-worker is able to share the burden of his workplace awareness.

It is often supposed that each individual priest-worker has to make a decision as to whether he will focus his ministry on his parish or on his workplace. My experience and that of others I have spoken with suggests that this is in fact a false dilemma. Most priest-workers find it impossible to say which of the two is the more important so since the two are not only mutually compatible but also interdependant and mutually reinforcing; their workplace experience needs to be underpinned by liturgy and in particular by the Eucharist which for most of them is a parochial activity, and in turn this liturgical experience underpins the exercise of their ministry at work. What characterises ordained ministry in the workplace, and what makes it a specific vocation, is a continuing commitment to job. Most priest-workers were workers before they were priests, and one of their greatest assets in their ministry is their years of job experence, prior perhaps their even having contemplated ordination; they have taken on a commitment to ordained ministry while retaining their commitment to their work. These two commitments have to jockey for priority, and are also in competition with other priorities, but reconciling their competing claims is a matter of personal organisation and self-discipline rather than anything that involves principle. The parish priest who meets his parishioners in their homes and in their home communities is aware of certain aspects of sin and is able to offer up these to God in intercession and at the Eucharist, but the priest-worker will be aware of aspects of sin which may well pass the parish priest by; it is important that these too should be offered up and God needs priests who understand them.

Ordained priesthood cannot, however, be constrained within definitions of roles and functions. The fact that priest-workers exist is evidence of the fact that the Church, at the very least, condones their existence, and it may be that one of the most important contributions of the non-stipendiary ministry is that it necessitates the asking of questions about what priesthood actually is. Answers are elusive. There is very little direct help to be had from the New Testament; I Timoth and Hebrews, the most relevant books, concentrate on exemplariness of character and on procedures so arcane as to have no obvious modern parallel. The terminology used in the ordination liturgy in the ASB is inspiring but capable of broad interpretation, for example, "You are to be messengers, watchmen and stewards of the Lord". Much of the ordination charge is to do with pastoral care, and once it is accepted that "the people to whom you are sent" is capable of including workplace colleagues, it becomes as applicable to priest-workers as to parochial clergy. There are direct requirements to proclaim the word of the Lord, to call hearers to repentance, to absolve sins in Christ's name and to declare the forgiveness of sins, and these may presumably be undertaken informally in the workplace as well as formally in a church. There is also the requirement to preside at the celebration of Holy Communion.

In the absence of any generally agreed description of the nature of ordained priesthood, there are three characteristics of it that are worth exploring in some detail. The first is that ordination is an office conferred by the Church, the second is that it imples a certain minimal level of spiritual awareness and closeness to God, and the third is that it implies at least a minimal degree of obligation to spread the good news of Christ's Kingdom and to enable other people to benefit through becoming aware of God's pervasive love and of the opportunity for redemption.

First, priesthood is an office conferred by the Church. The implications of this are threefold; first that ordination implies acceptance of the Church's discipline, second that ordination carries with it an authority conferred by the Church, and third, on the other side of the coin, that ordination is not conferred by the world which means that priesthood carries with it no special privileges or locus outside the Church community. The Anglican Church is hierarchical, and ordination requires the ordained person to submit himself to episcopal authority. Ordination implies different sorts of obedience in other denominations, but essential to it in every case is some sort of externally imposed discipline. The implications of this are clear enough in some areas but extremely vague in others, and in any event the mechanism by which this obedience is monitored and enforced is not clear at all. The requirement of obedience is most clear in respect of liturgical and sacramental procedures, most obviously in relation to services that happen in church buildings but presumably also in relation to what goes on in less formal settings. The requirement is also clear in respect of the orthodoxy of the Christian doctrine that is is proclaimed, though in workplaces what is proclaimed tends to be applied doctrine rather than pure doctrine and the orthodoxy of this is harder to measure. The requirement also applies to personal conduct and morality, but it is difficult to see how accepted principles are to be applied to workplace behaviour or how this is to be monitored. The requirement also extends to personal spirituality, prayer and church attendance, and to a general obligation to proclaim the Gospel. The essential point, however, is that acceptance of ordination implies acceptance of the Church's discipline. Since the Church does not have eyes and ears in every workplace, this discipline insofar as it affects priest-workers can only be self-monitored and self-enforced. And since as an employee a priest-worker will also have accepted the discipline required by his employer, he will have to be aware of the ultimate possibility of the two becoming incompatible which would necessitate resignation from either his orders or his job.

Ordination also confers the Church's authority. This means that an ordained priest-worker is authorised to perform the liturgy and administer the sacraments both inside and outside church buildings. It also means that the pastoral care and evangelism undertaken by the priest-worker carry with it the Church's authority. In circumstances where the relationship between priestly activity and the Church is formal and obvious, the nature of this authority will be clear since the fact that the priest-worker has received the sacrament of ordination will be known and the implications of it generally accepted and understood. However in less formal circumstances and among people who have less understanding of or sympathy with Church procedures, the nature of this authority is more mysterious. It will be important first in that the priest-worker will know that he has it; this will enhance his self-confidence and it will be this self-confidence that communicates itself to his colleagues rather than the fact that he has had hands laid upon him by a bishop. And it will be important secondly in that he will be able to explain to the people he is with that he is with them by the authority of the Church. How meaningful this will be will depend on how effectively he is able to put it across and upon how willing his colleagues are to accept it; it is indubitably a factor of potential significance, though perhaps the significance will be appreciated by his colleagues more during subsequent reflection than at the time. And it will be important thirdly in that the priest-worker will know that he has the full backing of the Church in what he does. He will be able to draw upon what he has learned and experienced during his ordination training, he will be able to take his priestly experiences back to the church and clergy with whom he is associated for their support, and most important he will be able to enhance his priestly activity in the workplace through his personal reflection, prayer and participation in the Eucharist.

However it has to be remembered that the authority conferred by ordination is conferred by the Church and not by the world; people who reject the Church will reject also what ordination stands for, and will perceive a priest-worker solely in the light of their own preconceptions and prejudices. Priesthood carries with it no special privileges and no special locus in the secular world, and the priest-worker needs to appreciate that in order to be listened to he must earn respect. Saint Paul talks in I Corinthians chapter 4 of being a fool for Christ's sake; being prepared to appear foolish on occasions, indeed being prepared to feel foolish, is intrinsic to being a Christian, and even more so to being an ordained clergyman, and more so still to being a priest-worker since there are so many occasions when what being ordained implies appears so totally out of kilter with workplace culture. Being prepared to appear foolish is part of being prepared to be vulnerable; a priest-worker is very vulnerable both to ridicule and to the erosion of his priestliness under the pressure of the constant demands of work and the ever-present spirit of mammon. But this vulnerability is simultaneously his greatest strength because it demonstrates with such effective impact that Christianity is about values that require the turning of the other cheek and that priesthood is not lightly borne. Fortunately, however, the priest-worker has God and the Church behind him in support and has the special grace of ordination to sustain him.

The second characteristic of ordination is that it implies a certain level of spiritual awareness and of closeness to God. A

117

superficial assessment of Christianity's spiritual tradition might suggest a history of two contrasting modes, one in the world and one removed from it, in which case the spirituality of the workplace would need to find its place within the former. However the more closely the tradition is examined, the more this distinction seems to wither away. Saint Antony of Egypt and the other desert fathers of the fourth and fifth centuries, who might be expected to take their place at the unworldly end of the spectrum, were fully aware of the nature of worldliness and only too ready to offer supremely practical advice. The two Saint Theresas also shared this worldly awareness, the Spanish one demonstrating her practical wisdom in majestic authoratitive sweeps and the French one in a petit-point of tenderness. The point is that spirituality is not a movement away from the world in order to get closer to God, it is a process of getting closer to God in order to bring the world closer to God. This means that the priest-worker's awareness of the world of work is potentially an asset to spirituality because of the insights that he gains in the course of his experience. The only difficulty is that he is likely to be busy and within this busyness it may be hard to find opportunity for prayer. However if prayer can become an attitude as well as an activity, prayer in the workplace can become a continuing experience that both informs and feeds off what goes on. All employed Christians, indeed all Christians, need to pray. The relevance of this to priest-worker is that prayer is a requirement since it is a pre-requisite for priestliness; if workplace colleagues cannot look to the prayer-based spirituality of a priest-worker they will see nothing worth seeing and he will be letting them down.

Ordination also carries with it an obligation for evangelism, for bringing to all people the good news of God's love for his world, the bad news of the way in which this world is distorted by sin, and the good news of the means of redemption. The world of work within which the priest-worker exercises his ministry might seem a particularly unpromising context for evangelism, both because of the supremely rational nature of what goes on all day and the ever intrusive primacy of contractual requirements, and because a large majority of the people with whom he is in contact will have only a minimal understanding of the Christian tradition, while many of the practising Christians will see their beliefs as having little relevance to their workplace activity. But the fact that the context is unpromising does not remove the evangelistic obligation; it serves to heighten the challenge and increase the responsibility. However this responsibility is made in some sense less onerous by the fact that the evangelistic obligation is in large measure discharged merely by the priest-worker's priestly presence. If people in a workplace know that one of their colleagues is an ordained priest, this will in itself be a reminder of God's presence there. The French worker-priests in the 1940s and 50s were preoccupied by a vision of the industrial workforce having become cut off from the Church's activity, and they sought to remedy this merely by their presence on the shop floor and by their demonstrable sharing in what went on. They saw the workers as being no longer capable of comprehending the language in which the Church preached the Gospel, and saw their priestly presence as being a non-verbal language that was universally understandable. This priestly presence is in some ways easier for priest-workers today since the barriers of social class are in large measure removed; many of the French worker-priests were of middle-class origin making an effort to integrate themselves within a working-class culture. However virtually all of today's priest-workers are employed in an environment commensurate with their social aspirations and at a level appropriate to their secular skills; very few slum it.

The evangelism of the priest-worker, then, comprises first that of indicating to people that their workplace has within it an authorised presence of the Church, secondly that of demonstrating a Christian life-style warts and all, and thirdly that of offering an opportunity for people to make use of as they choose. None of these require that he take any initiative beyond that of making his priesthood known. However on top of this there is scope for initiative, by way of providing pastoral care and of steering conversations so that the spiritual dimension of predicaments can at least be aired.

The growing number of priest-workers represents both an increasing number of priests choosing to exercise their ministry in secular employment and also an increasing number of people in secular employment choosing to seek ordination. In spite of the difficulties that the non-stipendiary priesthood causes for Church organisation and discipline and for congregations who have to relate to "spare-time" clergy, the effect is to bring the Church and the world of work closer together enabling the Church to learn more about work and enabling workers to learn more about the Church. This does not in itself solve the problems that exist at the interface between Christianity and paid employment, but it does mean that the relevant questions are inevitably being asked by more people and with greater urgency, and this cannot but make the emergence of helpful answers more likely.

9

Integration Three: The Church in the Workplace

The opening chapter of this book drew attention to the difficulty of integrating the experiences of Christian belief and the experiences of paid employment within a single framework, particularly the difficulty inherent in reconciling institutional values with the values implied by the Sermon on the Mount. The role of the Church is to reveal and reassert God's purpose in the world and it thus has a priority of commitment to the values of the Sermon on the Mount, but Christianity, perhaps to a greater extent than any of the other great world religions, is committed to the world as it exists and has never preached world rejection. A significant ingredient of the world as it exists at this particular moment in time is paid institutional employment, and this chapter looks at the necessity of the Church absorbing into itself the reality of paid employment, complete with its value system and all that it stands for, instead of standing aloof from it. And it also looks at the benefits that might result if this were actually to happen. "Church" is always a difficult word to define, but in this chapter it is used to mean three things, either separately as indicated by the context, or more often all three simultaneously. The first is the Church gathered locally, in the sense of the clergy and congregation of a particular place of worship. The second is the Church gathered nationally in the sense of the sum of all bishops, clergy, and congregations. And the third is the Church as the body of Christ, the actual embodiment within the world of the remembrance and continuing presence to Jesus which the local and national gathering strive more or less successfully to become.

Chapter 3 made the distinction between religious awareness and rational activity and saw paid employment as being for the most part rational activity. The Church, in contrast, is concerned primarily with religious awareness and with developing individual people's capacity for it, first by showing them that they have it, then by nurturing it and directing it aright, and then by providing a context within which it can find expression. If the

121

distinction between religous awareness and rational activity were absolute there would be little scope for dialogue and indeed no need for it, but Chapter 3 also made the point that the fact that people behave rationally some of the time doesn't stop them from being spiritual beings. Effective work, however rational, is a deeply satisfying spiritual experience, so the Church would wish to see the scope for effective work increased, and conversely the absence of the opportunity for effective work is deeply detrimental to the spirit which gives the Church a locus in articulating the spiritually damaging effects of soul-destroying jobs and of chronic unemployment. And experiences at work cannot but exert a spiritual influence on the individuals concerned. The nature of this influence will vary greatly and be either positive or negative; a chance encounter with another person or the effect of a particular assignment can deepen spiritual insights, while bad experiences such as an inhumane assignment or being victimised or scapegoated or made redundant or sacked can engender bitterness or cynicism. This influence may be cumulative as the value system of a particular workplace heightens or erodes a person's spiritual awareness over time. And institutions are capable of enormous impact on the lives of people outside them both on those who are at the receiving end of what the institution provides and on the population at large who are affected by the institution's general ethos; people who work within the institution concerned will inevitably know about the spiritual dimension of this impact and be affected by it.

The Church needs to take all this on board, but its reaction will need to be circumscribed since it is not in the business of confronting rational activity with more rational activity; its concern is with the impact of rational activity upon individual and corporate spirituality. This may on occasion require that the Church speak out, but this public reaction will need to be confined to statements about spiritual impact and not extend to statements about how institutions ought to manage their affairs since this would be at risk of trespassing upon the autonomy of technique. In many instances the Church's only appropriate reaction to people's work experiences and to the impact of institutions will be just to pray; it is important that the Church appreciate both that this sort of prayer is impossible without an understanding of the world of work and that pragmatic impotence does not imply spiritual inaction. There are many ways in which this intercessionary activity can happen, perhaps through a group of Christians meeting within a particular workplace, perhaps through congregations drawing upon the institutional experiences of their individual members, and perhaps through the Church nationally demonstrating an interest.

All this is by the way of a plea that the Church should be doing what it ought to be doing anyway. However if the Church were to start doing it effectively there would be a number of probable consequences which might initially seem threatening but which would be likely to have a number of unexpectedly beneficial results in the long term. The first consequence would be a broadening of the Church's concern. People's lives would be seen in a broader context which would include an awareness of their experiences in paid employment and their experiences of being at the receiving end of institutional impact. Parochial clergy and their pastoral care teams are probably already aware of this impact insofar as its effects are catastrophic; they will know if a person has been sacked or made redundant, and will see this as an event that requires pastoral intervention. They will also know whether a particular person has just been discharged from hospital or is having difficulty with social security or with social services or with the housing authority, and will do their best to help. But they are unlikely to be much concerned with the more mundane effects of institutional employment. My experience of Church discussion, whether it be in the aftermath of Sunday services or slightly more formally in house discussion groups, is that it is very rare for people to feel happy talking about their work or attempting to bring to bear any of the insights that their work experience may have given them on spiritual matters. This reticence means that potentially valuable opportunities are lost both for new lights to be shed upon Christian doctrine by it being viewed from the standpoint of paid employment, and for any attitudes that may have been distorted by the experience of paid employment to be aired and corrected. If work experience were to be placed more firmly on the Church's agenda much would be gained.

The second consequence would be a fuller appreciation of the

Church's role. The distinction between practical activity and spirituality is an important one and the Church's concern is primarily with the latter, but an increased awareness of where the boundary lies would lead to an increased awareness of the spiritual imperatives to which the Church is committed. A deeper appreciation of the fact that in many instances direct action by the Church is inappropriate would lead to a more ready acceptance of the Church's pragmatic impotence. This in turn would increase its awareness of its intercessional responsibilities and perhaps in turn increase its confidence in its intercessional effectiveness.

The third consequence would be to increase the Church's awareness of the predicaments of non-churchgoers. The difference between a church congregation and a workplace community is that in the former the ethos is determined by believers while in the latter it is determined by non-believers, and the workplace for most committed Christians is the most important point of contact with the non-believing ethos. Most Christians start from the assumption that non-churchgoers would benefit from increased contact with committed churchgoers, but they need also to appreciate that committed churchgoers have a great deal to learn from non-believers.

And the fourth consequence would be the broadening of the Church's horizons to ecompass the full spectrum of the human condition. There may have been times in the dim and distant past when the Church was at the forefront of social and attitudinal change, but this is certainly not the case in this country today except in a few marginal and discrete areas. The pace of change is dictated for the most part by what goes on in workplaces. Changes in income and workplace practices affect the attitudes of individual employees, which in turn determine how they view their homes, their communities and their leisure activities; the new technologies that are the output of workplaces affect the whole nature of people's lives and their attitudes towards them, and the impact of the major institutions affects the structure of society as a whole. Only by keeping abreast of all this can the Church hope to demonstrate the need for a strong spiritual framework within which such change can be accommodated, and only by understanding the nature of such changes can the Church fulfill its responsibility for providing such a framework.

So often going to a Sunday morning service leaves one with a doleful impression of the Church as an insignificant backwater where a few marginal or neurotic people cling to a nostalgic hope that what was relevant yesterday will be relevant tomorrow, and that the world is leaving the Church further and further behind.

What can the Church learn from the world of work, and how can this learning happen? The first lesson is corrective. The essence of sin is self-centredness, a pre-occupation with the requirements of the ego which distracts from concerns of more lasting importance. One of the purposes of the Church is to provide an escape route from ego-domination; by revealing the path that leads towards identification with God, it can encourage people to take a God's-eye view of things and see them objectively and in proportion. However the Church sometimes has difficulty in signposting this path because, in its concern for individuals, it inevitably has to take account of their egotistic needs. Very often the people who go to Church go there in search of a haven for their egos which may have been severely damaged in the course of their journey through the world. The pastoral concern of the Church is with the healing and restoring of damaged egos, but a preoccupation with this pastoral task may be at the expense of the next and more important stage with is helping people to bypass the demands of their egos and so become closer to the common core of humanity and of creation which is God. A congregation is a gathering of like-minded people and, like all gatherings of like-minded people, its collective culture is at risk of becoming divorced from external reality and the consequent distortions are at risk of becoming self-reinforcing. Chapter 3 quoted Arnold Toynbee's image of the source of religious awareness being the subconscious emotional abyss and his appreciation of the subconscious being also the source of destructive neuroses that are at risk of being mistaken for religion. Some of the preoccupations of groups of Christians, whether they be with breast-beating admissions of sin or with the tinkling bells of ritual, would benefit enormously from a healthy injection of non-churchgoing concerns like hedonistic enjoyment and being successful in business. The perspective of the world of work is not the only one that offers the necessary corrective of reality-based objectivity; the historian's viewpoint enables people to dissociate themselves from the subjectivity in which they are trapped by the circumstances of time and place, and the research scientist's viewpoint, with its emphasis on value-free empirical observation, has the same effect. But the institutional viewpoint is equally effective and is one to which the Church has readier access; it sees people not in terms of the needs of their egos but in terms of their potential and actual contribution to the achievement of objectives. The world of work is concerned with rational activity and the rational viewpoint is a limited one, but it has its usefulness particularly if what is needed is an injection of reality at a time when pastoral preoccupation is at risk of swamping a concern for spiritual development.

The second reason why the Church needs to learn from the world of work is because congregations, if they are to be in any way successful in the task of spreading the good news of the Gospel to those who are deaf to it, need to have at least some understanding of the nature of the deafness. The Church has tended to see non-churchgoers as being particularly ripe for evangelism at times when they are in trouble, for example after a bereavement or during family ructions or after redundancy or other difficulties at work. No doubt this is shrewd psychology but it includes a not-insignificant hint of exploitation, and the Church would be greatly helped by a deeper understanding of why the people who are being evangelised were non-churchgoers in the first place. Such deeper understanding could not but be helpful in the more obvious task of spreading the good news to people who are enjoying themselves and being successful, and a sensible place to start would be through listening carefully and sensitively to what people in paid employment have to say.

And the third area where the Church has something to learn has to do with language. It is very difficult for human beings to absorb and understand their spiritual experiences before first translating them into words and symbols. The language in which spirituality has traditionally been expressed originates in the main from two sources, home and work. The experiences of home, of the marriage relationship, of bringing up children, and of care during illness, infirmity and old age, have always been used as metaphors for spiritual truths, and still are because the attitudes and tasks involved have not essentially changed. But the experiences of work have changed radically. Many of the perennial spiritual truths of the Bible are expressed in a language firmly rooted in the work and life-style of the Fertile Crescent at the time when it was written. Many of the Old Testament metaphors are repeated in the New, and the everyday experiences they were drawn from continued to be shared by generation after generation of Christian people. The language of Cranmer's Prayer Book and the Authorised Version of the Bible also had this strong bond with the lives that people actually led. But now, within the space of a few generations, this bond has been almost totally severed. The language of spiritual truth is no longer the language of everyday life. This means that attempts to articulate spiritual experiences have either to use language and modes of thought that are no longer common currency, which creates the risk of equating spirituality with nostalgic escapism, or they have to be the outcome of a heroic personal effort to find a new language and a new mode of thought, which in turn is at risk of being idiosyncratic since it is not nourished by tradition. In the words of the French worker-priest Emile Poulat, "Tradition was the norm of the concrete activity in which the spiritual experience of men took root. It is this foundation, which Christianity always used, which is now suddenly lacking. However competent a Christian may be in the new disciplines (of science and technology), he remains, through his faith, bound to a form of culture with which the rest of his life has ceased to be nourished, and to which unbelievers have no reason to remain attached". This puts an urgent responsibility on the Church to strengthen its contacts with the workplace, because it is within the workplace that much of this new language is being developed and much of this new culture created. It is important not only as an aid in reaching out to non-churchgoers, but also as a means of helping employed believers who already go to church but who hear the Gospel proclaimed in terms that may have little relevance to their first-hand experience.

An illustration may be helpful. My understanding of Jesus has given me an insight into the role of the shepherd, and not vice versa. My relationship with the few shepherds that I have ever actually come across has had as its starting point the New Testament descriptions of what shepherds used to do. Previous generations were presumably able to understand the point that

Jesus was making when he said "I am the good shepherd" because their first-hand knowledge of the role of the shepherd gave them an immediate insight. I, on the other hand, because I have no such first-hand experience, have to make three very difficult steps; first I have to attempt to understand what Jesus is saying by relating it to my own very different experience, then I have to use this as a basis for understanding the role of the shepherd, and then I have to apply to Jesus this understanding of the shepherd I have just arrived at in order to clarify my understanding of what he is saying. It would have been much easier for me if Jesus had said "I am a good personnel manager". I am not going so far as to suggest that the Gospel be rewritten using this sort of terminology, though attempts to rewrite bits of it can be both helpful and hilarious; the point is that the world of work is now the origin of may of the metaphors that people use as a means of understanding their predicaments, and these metaphors are no longer linked to the metaphors of spiritual tradition. It is unrealistic to plead for the immediate creation of a new spiritual language since traditions by definition need to evolve over time, but the Church needs urgently to recognise and accept a specific role as the interpreter between the language of traditional spirituality and the language of present day experience, and it can only do this if it speaks both languages with equal fluency. To learn the latter it needs to be in constant contact with those who are in institutional employment.

My contacts with my workplace colleagues over the years have convinced me that the majority of them are as aware of God as most churchgoing Christians even though they may not attribute his name to their experiences. They have a sense of their value and importance as individuals even though they may not describe it as being loved by God, and they have a sense of what they need to do to maintain their personal integrity even though they may not call it doing God's will. They have a sense of what it means to compromise their personal integrity even though they may not call it sin, and they understand how to recuperate from it even though they may not call it repentance and redemption. They appreciate the importance of their commitment to their work, to their families, to bringing up their children and to caring for elderly relatives even though they may not describe it as worship. They are aware that there are aspects of their experience that are of deeper significance than their mundane routines even though they may not choose to describe them as being close to God, and they understand and practise prayer even if they happen to call it taking the dog for a walk. This isn't true of all of them, of course; there are some who have got their priorities badly wrong, perhaps pursuing particular ambitions at the expense of other areas of their experience, and some who have discrete blockages about particular aspects of reality, and some who are so deeply unhappy that everything around them becomes distorted and destructive. But then this is true of churchgoing Christians also. Some of these unhappy people get back to normal by means of the honesty about themselves that comes from growing older and wiser, and some as a result of a traumatic experience that cannot be ignored. And some remain unredeemed.

The point is that Christians do not have a monopoly in God's love and are not unique in their awareness of God's working, and it is this shared awareness that provides the contact point between Christians and non-Christians at work and elsewhere. Very often these non-Christians considered Christianity at some previous stage of their lives, and the reasons why they rejected it or abandoned it were that the picture of it that they received was a travesty of what Christian belief is really about. Some were shown Christianity as morally censorious, whereas what they wanted was the freedom to be themselves. Some were shown the Church as a group which excludes those who are unwilling or unable to behave in certain ways or follow particular procedures, whereas what they wanted was to be in touch with everyone. Some were shown a preoccupation with sin and guilt, whereas what they wanted was the means to become happy. Some attended Church and failed to understand the meaning of what went on, whereas what they wanted was something with a demonstrable sense of purpose. Some were put off by what they saw as a preoccupation with symbols and rituals that were unrelated to their experience, whereas what they wanted was something that would have meaning in the lives they actually lead. The Church needs to speak to people like these both because of what it has to offer them and, even more so, because of what it can learn from such a dialogue which might show it how to put its own house in order. And the workplace is as good a place as any in which to start, because it is where Christians and non-Christians most easily rub shoulders in the context of genuinely shared activity.

And the Church needs confidence that what it has on offer is worthwhile. It is significant that Christians call themselves after Jesus Christ; God is there for anybody and everybody to be aware of as best they are able, but what is special to Christianity is Jesus as a means of increasing this awareness and of ensuring that the awareness is genuine, and as a means of getting closer to God. What Jesus demonstrated is that God became man that therefore man might become God. The incarnation of Jesus is proof that God exists within each and everyone of us, the teaching of Jesus shows each and everyone of us what God in man looks like in practice, and the death and resurrection of Jesus shows each and every one of us how our imperfections are not of necessity barriers to the identification of man and God. What the Church has on offer, and it is an offer worth making because it is an offer worth accepting, is the Eucharist, not just as a reminder of all this, but as a regular opportunity for incorporating into ourselves its ongoing truth.

10

Ultimate Integration: The Kingdom of God

In the Lord's Prayer, we ask that God's Kingdom might come. Our understanding of what would actually happen if this prayer were to be granted is based on Jesus' parables about the nature of the Kingdom; love would triumph like the tree that grew from the mustard seed, and sin and all its consequential damage would wither away. The kingdom is not a description of any present or past state of affairs, except perhaps in the Garden of Eden before man developed the gift of free will and therefore the capacity for sin, nor is it a description of any probable future state of affaris. Nevertheless, when we are in the presence of love we experience momentarily what the Kingdom is like, and these momentary glimpses are sufficient to motivate us at least some of the time towards bringing the Kingdom about to the best of our own constrained and limited ability. The Church is a perpetual reminder that humanity has within itself the capacity for redemption and that the Kingdom is capable of being realised, albeit in this life only in small doses.

The parables make clear two important aspects of the Kingdom; one is that it involves everybody and not merely any particular race, sect, congregation or group, and the other is that it involves the whole of our lives and not any particular part of it like the part we spend in church. Peter Baelz introduces his chapter on the theology of the Kingdom in the anthology he edited called *Ministers of the Kingdom* with a quotation from Bishop John Robinson: "Just as the New Testament bids us have as high a doctrine the ministry as we like so long as our doctrine of the Church is higher, so it commands us to have as high a doctrine of the Church as we may, provided our doctrine of the Kingdom is higher". What this means is that however much importance we attach to our Christian practices, we need to see them as merely a part of the activity of the universal Church, and however much importance we attach to the work of the Church, we need to see it as merely a part of God's activity in the world.

Looked at from this perspective, work, whether paid or

unpaid, is just one of the many things that human beings do, and just one of the many ways open to us for self-discovery and self-expression. God watches us when we are in our workplaces just as he watches us when we are in our homes or on holiday or in church, and he sees us getting some things right and some things wrong, and either learning or failing to learn from both. There is joy when we get things right and when we succeed in learning, and this joy is felt by God whether or not we feel it too, and there is pain when we get things wrong and when we fail to learn, and this pain is felt by God whether or not we feel it too. God gives us ample opportunities for loving and for being loved by other people, and these other people are as likely to be our workplace colleagues as they are to be members of our families or of our congregations. He gives us ample opportunities for doing his will, and these opportunities are as likely to arise in our workplaces as they are in our homes or when we are engaged in church activities. The difference between paid employment all the other things that human beings do is merely that during the course of paid employment we are subjected to a particular set of constraints and presented with a particular set of challenges, both dictated by the nature of the work in which we are engaged. But then everything that human beings do is constrained, both in terms of what we have to do and what we have not to do; at home we have to get the cooking and the housework done and there is little scope for playing in an orchestra, while in church we have to concentrate on the liturgy and it would be a little awkward if we wanted to get on with our correspondence and type some letters. And the challenges we are presented with are complex wherever we may be; it is as difficult to identify the Christian way of cooking a turkey as it is to identify the Christian way of entering figures in a ledger. And looked at from this point of view, all the things that human beings do become equally sacred since all of them are watched over by God and have as their ultimate purpose the discovery and realisation of what it is that God means human beings to be; cooking, housework, typing letters, playing second violin and everything we do in paid employment are just as much a part of this process of discovery and realisation as what we do in church.

Paid employment is just one aspect of individual people's lives, however absorbing it may be and whatever constraints it may impose, and the lives of individual people are just one aspect of God's purpose in creation. To paraphrase Bishop Robinson, it doesn't matter how important to us our paid employment may be so long as we see it as merely a part of our lives as a whole, and it doesn't matter how much importance we attach to our own lives so long as we are capable of seeing them as just one life among all the others in the total context of creation. The constraints imposed by paid employment don't matter so long as they don't act as blinkers against a broader vision of God's purpose, and our responses to the challenges presented in paid employment don't matter so long as they are not detrimental to the working out of that purpose. What Christian belief adds to paid employment is the broader vision of God's purpose which helps us to get our paid employment into the right perspective, and what Church membership adds is the inevitability of this purpose being perpetually revealed and reasserted.

This book takes its title from the parable in St Matthew chapter 22, and the book's opening chapter acknowledged the temptation to make a distinction between the things that are appropriate for rendering unto Caesar and the things that are appropriate for rendering unto God. If we take the present day equivalents of Caesar as being our secular employing institutions, there are indeed things which it is appropriate for us as employees to render unto our own particular Caesars; our employers demand from us a significant proportion of our time, of our energy, of our creativity, and of our loyalty and commitment. However what I hope this book has shown is that what is rendered unto Caesar in the first instance is rendered ultimately to God; our employing institutions are merely the first-line recipients of our offering to God of our workplace experience. The work we do in the context of our paid employment is God's work, whether or not we attribute to him the credit; all Caesars, our own and Jesus' Tiberias, are merely elements in the sacred immensity of God's purpose.

Praise from the Critics

Peter Levi
The Holy Gospel of John
A New Translation

"Once the reader has become accustomed to the rhythmic if somewhat staccato effect produced by so stylish a fidelity to the evangelist's own technique, he will find himself hooked—perhaps at a deeper level of intimacy with the word of John than ever previously experienced".

Gerard Noel in *The Sunday Telegraph*

"Peter Levi, poet and critic, is a fine classical scholar. His prose is pure and elegant and he can sense how rugged is the Koine (gutter) Greek of the first Christians, but that is its point. Matthew, Mark and Luke are to follow. Can he keep it up? Let's hope so".

Martin Jarrett-Kerr in *The Guardian*

"Peter Levi is a classical scholar, Professor of Poetry at Oxford and himself a poet. With this background one would expect his translation of St John's Gospel to be characterised by 'fine writing'. Professor Levi's purpose is quite different. He wants to keep as close as possible to the original Greek, to the extent of reproducing its roughness. Together with this he aims at the greatest possible simplicity". Richard Harries in *The Church Times*

"We hear the Gospel with the freshness with which its first hearers received it". Michael Hinsley in *The Church of England Newspaper*

"What a beautiful translation this is. It is the work of a poet and if there is any Gospel that needs a poet it is surely John". Edwin Robertson, formerly Assistant Head of Religious Broadcasting, BBC

"The chief advantage will be for those who would like to have a feel for the original language but have not even a smattering of Greek".

Peter Wortley in *The Baptist Times*

ISBN 1 85093 027 9 Hardback £5.95

Another Outstanding Book from Churchman

Peter Mayhew
Unemployment under the Judgement of God

"It is a lovely book. Peter Mayhew's goodness of purpose shines through the pages. It will also be a useful book if it stimulates each of us to personal action providing a job rather than just telling the Government what to do.".   John Garnett, Director of The Industrial Society
in the *Oxford Diocesan Magazine*

"Peter Mayhew makes it plain in this very readable book that unemployment is not a cold—it is a cancer. It calls for ruthless surgery, not by one man but by everyone in society."   *The Baptist Times*

"We need all the new thinking we can develop and all the urgency we can muster in facing and tackling unemployment. Father Mayhew has had a go. Read which he has to say and see if you can do better."
The Bishop of Durham

"(this book) is by a retired priest, formerly a headmaster and much else and latterly the chaplain of an Anglican convent in Oxford. He is a youthfully passionate writer who fills his pages with people and facts encountered very far from any convent. Now in his seventies he has a vision of the next century."   The Provost of Southwark in the *Church Times*

"Verdict: read and lend Mayhew."   The Reverend the Lord Beaumont
in the *Catholic Herald*

"This book will particularly interest those concerned with labour relations, the plight of the unemployed or social theology, but it is aimed essentially at anyone with both a job and a conscience."   Peter Cox
in *British Book News*

"Peter Mayhew has written a thoughtful and thought-provoking book which deserves a wide readership. It is deeply concerned with people and the community and, for this sin, will probably be seen as a clerical intrusion into the world of politics by certain elected representatives. It is to be hoped that Peter Mayhew and David Jenkins, to whom the book is dedicated, continue to make such intrusions and address with purpose the major moral issues of our time which belong to no one estate, least of all that which is the most powerful."   Paul Rathkey in the
*Jim Conway Memorial Foundation Trade Union Report,
Volume 6, No. 7*

ISBN 1 85093 025 2 Large Format Paperback £6.95